Flexible, Missional Constitution/Bylaws

In One Day, Not Two Years

Alan C. Klaas
Cheryl D. Klaas

Mission Growth Publishing
Oak Park, IL

Mission Growth Publishing books are available through most bookstores. They are also available by using the order form printed at the end of the book or by visiting:

www.MissionGrowth.org

Library of Congress Catalog Card #00-109752

ISBN 0-9702314-1-5

CONTENTS

1. Overview   1

2. The World Has Changed   3

3. The Way People Work Has Changed   8

4. Structuring Congregations Has Changed   11

5. Creating the Event   20

6. Drafting a New Constitution   26

7. Drafting New Bylaws   31

8. Bringing Constitution and Bylaws Together   34

9. Transition From Current to New   36

10. Operating Procedures   38

11. Operating Policies   43

12. Spiritual/Ministry Development   48

Appendix A: Constitution and Bylaws of St. Paul Church   51

Appendix B: Draft Constitution and Bylaws   56

Appendix C: Other Wordings of Constitutions and Bylaws   63

Appendix D: Notes to Subgroups   74

Appendix E: Draft Policy Manuals   80

Appendix F: Notes for Event Facilitator   88

ACKNOWLEDGMENTS

We want to thank the hundreds of congregations and their leaders who have pioneered new ways of structuring and organizing churches. These individuals realized that the world in which their congregations exist is not the same one that existed when their constitutions and bylaws were drafted or copied from others. These leaders understood that the way in which congregations currently function is different from how churches worked the days of the churched culture. They paved the way for thousands of congregations to follow in creating flexible and missional constitutions and bylaws appropriate to achieving the Great Commission.

We are grateful to John Carver for his ground-breaking book *Boards That Make a Difference*. The insights it presents into the mechanics of leadership in not-for-profit organizations have helped many thousands of charitable and religious organizations. His perspectives on the roles that senior leadership boards should and should not play are making a significant difference in the ministry success of churches and church-related organizations.

We are especially grateful to our mentor and friend, Kennon Callahan. All of Kennon's writing and teaching on congregations are filled with hundreds of practical insights into how to structure and lead local churches. His two landmark books on church leadership, *Twelve Keys to an Effective Church* and *Effective Church Leadership*, are filled with insights on the mission and structure of congregations.

We appreciate the churches that have allowed us to be helpful as they planned their future and created the structures needed to turn those dreams into reality. We particularly appreciate those churches in which the specific process of developing a new constitution and bylaws in one day was tested and improved.

We owe special thanks to Drew Bryan for his work in final edit and to Tammy Hildreth for the cover design. Finally, we want to thank the good folks at Whitehall Printing for their work in bringing the whole effort together in the printing process.

Chapter 1
Overview

Most congregations have a constitution and bylaws document of thirty or more pages. It details the administrative structure of the church, how officials are elected, and ascribes authority to make decisions.

Most existing constitutions and bylaws are rigid and inflexible. Changing them requires a daunting effort normally not attempted except at intervals of ten or twenty years.

Many congregations are experiencing difficulty complying with their constitution and bylaws. Required positions go unfilled. Nominating committees struggle to recruit candidates even for the key officer positions. Often congregations find it is becoming harder and harder to get anything done.

Frankly, most congregations have too many boards and committees and too many people on those boards and committees. In addition, the way the boards and committees are structured automatically eliminates larger percentages of the members or frequent attenders from participating.

This book describes a way out of the mess. The book explains how to create a "missional constitution" to replace the "complex structural constitution." It describes a flexible structure rather than a rigid structure. Following the book's suggestions will give the congregation a flexible and missional document of about ten pages.

Most importantly, following the suggested procedures allows the congregation to create its new constitution in …

… one Saturday, not the normal two years.

This claim may seem preposterous, but it works. Most members already have a sense that the current constitution is inhibiting the mission and ministry of the church. Active members are aware that the structure is becoming more difficult to maintain. Virtually all are interested in finding a better way.

Because of this, it is not necessary to spend a great deal of time investigating, explaining, and "selling" the need for a new constitution and bylaws. The difficulty of the current structure coupled with the simplicity of the suggested draft makes a compelling combination.

This book achieves three goals. First, it provides the underlying principles for developing a new constitution and bylaws. Second, it describes a simple way of structuring the document. Third, it spells out the specific procedures to follow in creating the new constitution and bylaws in one day.

Some will be tempted to adopt a strategy that involves several months of study, or even a year or two to complete. They are free to choose that strategy—even though it is not necessary or helpful.

Some will be tempted to shortcut or change the suggested procedures, which could backfire. Church members appreciate the rapid pace of the described process, but will resist if they feel themselves forced or "railroaded."

Full presentation of the background material scripted in Chapters 2 – 4 is critical. These chapters contain three explanations that are important to members' understanding and acceptance of the remainder of the process. The meeting leader (facilitator) is encouraged to present or even read the text and to use overhead projection visuals of the key points. (A Microsoft® Word document of the text and a Microsoft®

PowerPoint® presentation of the key points are available.)

Chapter 5 lists the activities used to develop a draft of the new constitution and bylaws in one day. (It can be adapted for use in two or three sessions.) The step-by-step explanation guides the event organizers through everything needed to create a successful event.

Chapter 6 explains how to help the congregation make the relatively few key decisions needed for the new constitution. It is not necessary during the event to discuss the specific wording of the constitution. It is enough to make about ten key decisions.

Chapter 7 contains the procedures for creating the bylaws. It is a simple approach that accomplishes a great deal in a short period of time.

Chapter 8 leads the assembly through a concluding activity in which the specific wording of the constitution and bylaws are drafted.

Chapter 9 explains how to make the transition from the current constitution to the new one.

The last two chapters are critical to the successful implementation of a congregation's new structure. Chapter 10 suggests a specific approach to the actual functioning of the leadership under the new constitution. It provides a place to begin, after which modifications will be needed to better fit the specific situation in the congregation.

Chapter 11 is not part of the structure of the new constitution and bylaws. And yet it is the heart and soul of helping the congregation function as a mission outpost on its local mission field. This chapter describes the importance of, and a way forward with, a formal program of spiritual development of individual members. It completes the circle started in the second chapter's explanation of why congregations struggle under their current constitutions.

John 3:16 says, "For God so loved the world." It does not say, "For God so loved the church." This is a key distinction between most current constitutions and the one proposed in this book. Current constitutions were written with the institution as the center of people's lives. The new constitution is written with the Great Commission as the center of people's lives. In current

times, the healthiest churches are those focused on the Great Commission, not on their own survival.

Chapter 11 provides an overview of the basic principles of the spiritual development process that undergirds the new constitution. Those who choose to ignore Chapter 11 will limit the success of their new structures.

The content of the suggested flexible, missional constitution and bylaws does not come from the authors. It comes from the constitutions and bylaws of several dozen churches experiencing Great Commission ministries. The background so critical to accepting this new approach (Chapters 2 – 4) comes from studies conducted by the authors and many others comparing thousands of thriving and struggling congregations. The specific method of accomplishing so much in only one day was developed, tested, and refined by the authors of this book.

Chapter 2
The World Has Changed

(Note: Inserted into the text of this book are notes to the facilitator of the one-day event in which the congregation creates a draft of a flexible, missional constitution and bylaws. These notes are printed in italics.

Also inserted in Chapters 2, 3, 4 and 6 is **text in bold type.** *These are cues signifying the next slide or line within a slide of overhead projector slides or PowerPoint slides that can be used when presenting the text. The slides are available on a 3½ inch diskette—see Appendix G.)*

Constitution and Bylaws

Church **constitutions and bylaws** exist within the context of the times in which they were written, approved, and amended. Most congregations have constitutions and bylaws written or copied from others written during the days of the churched culture.

Most constitutions and bylaws are a long list of **rules and regulations, conditions and stipulations, policies and procedures** that were effective in their day. They were developed during a time when people appreciated extensive structure and were willing to work within that structure.

However, **the world has changed.** In former times it was "the thing to do to go to church." Participating in a local congregation was automatic for a person of faith. We celebrate the many things that were accomplished during those days of the churched culture.

But **the day of the churched culture is over and the day of mission has come.** In present times, we live on a vast mission field of unchurched people. Going to church is no longer the thing to do.

In fact, **North America is currently among the largest mission fields on the planet.** Fifty to eighty percent of every community is **effectively unchurched. Foreign countries are now sending missionaries to the United States.** Some people estimate that the United States is now the third largest recipient of foreign missionaries.

In the days of the churched culture, the term "mission field" generally meant Africa, Central or South America, and New Guinea. Sometimes mission meant prison ministry, soup kitchens, and homes for wayward children. The term "mission field" implied someplace distant from most churches.

The mission field has moved to the church's property boundaries. Between fifty and eighty percent of the church's neighbors are effectively unchurched. In some urban areas that percentage is even higher. Some congregations remind themselves of this reality by placing signs at the exit doors and driveways that read, "You are now entering the mission field." These congregations attempt to help themselves remember that God has placed them as a "mission outpost on a local mission field."

Churched Culture – Mission Outpost

The implications of this change from a churched culture to a mission field have profoundly affected how congregations are organized. Interestingly, many of the structural characteristics that were strengths in the churched culture have become limitations on the mission field.

There is a long list of differences between churched culture churches and mission outposts. The differences are all connected, one feeding the next and all related to each other.

A churched culture structure focuses on **functions** to be achieved. Tasks needed to be accomplished and structures were created to complete those tasks.

On a mission field, the emphasis is on the **relational** aspects. The needed activities are achieved, but the emphasis is on relationships between people and mission rather than on lines of reporting responsibility.

During the churched culture, tasks were accomplished by many **committees** conducting monthly meetings. Often large numbers of people were on each committee, usually to assure that nobody became too powerful.

Often the members of the committees were there because they felt a sense of responsibility, or "nobody else would do it." Many of these individuals were only marginally interested in the activity assigned to the committee.

On a mission field, **action teams** containing the appropriate number of people accomplish most of a church's work. They meet when they need to meet and do not meet when it is not necessary. Task force members volunteer for the group and are motivated to serve in the ministry area that matches their gifts and interests.

When things become difficult under the churched culture structure, the normal response is a call to "**work harder**." Unfortunately, when people work harder they simply become more tired. Tired people easily become grumpy people. Tired and grumpy people may not be the most effective ambassadors for the congregation or Christ's work on earth.

The mission outpost response is to "**work smarter**." When the congregation is having difficulty completing a particular activity, serious consideration is given to whether the activity should even continue. If it should continue, the solution is sought by finding a different way to accomplish the activity.

Churched culture churches spend much of their leadership meeting time and most of their planning time dealing with **weaknesses** and problems. Commonly, the leadership meetings start with a financial report that indicates to the leaders that money is tight. Perceived lack of money causes leaders to set aside missional activities, or anything new, until income rises.

Planning meetings feature long lists of problems, weaknesses, challenges, and difficulties. These are usually printed on large sheets of paper and posted on the walls. Surrounded by problems, it is only natural that the meeting acquires a tone of defeat. In response, those gathered then identify grandiose problem-solving schemes that most deep down know will never work.

Mission outpost congregations focus on their **strengths** and are not intimidated by their problems. For example, a churched culture congregation in a low-income area often postpones ministry, waiting for others to bail them out. The opposite is a thriving mission outpost church in a low-income area that simply refuses to have its ministry limited by lack of money. It uses the gifts God has given it to accomplish realistic, missional goals.

Churched culture churches **fear mistakes**, and are organized to prevent mistakes. They would rather kill a new idea than take even a slight chance that the new idea will prove to be a mistake. In so doing, they limit themselves to their historical activities—even when those activities are no longer effective.

Creativity is the heart and soul of the activities of mission outpost congregations. They are eager, not reckless, to try **creative** new ideas. They empower small task forces and action teams to try new ministry activities and avoid second-guessing their decisions. They will have programs that do not work out, but those failed programs are celebrated as opportunities to learn.

Fear of mistakes is driven by a **fear of failure**. These two fears paralyze churched culture churches, condemning them to the "tried and true" activities used for years. Planning for next year always begins with repeating what was done the previous year, years, or decades.

In the days of the churched culture, the same activities were perceived to be effective year in and year out, for decades or lifetimes. A new activity that failed caused the people creating the idea to be criticized, sometimes ostracized, but always driven to avoid ever again suggesting anything new. More importantly, everyone else sees what happens to failed new ideas, and they resolve never to suggest anything new.

In most congregations, structure is created to prevent failures. Structures that prevent failures also prevent anything new.

Mission outpost congregations are willing to **risk** new ideas. There are high levels of trust and eagerness to see if a new idea will be effective. If the structure limits the new idea, then the structure is changed.

The result of fearing failure and mistakes is that the church only **reacts** to problems. The functional structure, committees, and preoccupation with weaknesses all work together with fear of mistakes or failure. The congregation makes itself helpless to do anything but react to problems. Thus, the whole system perpetuates itself, creating of a bland stew of sameness.

Mission outpost congregations **proactively** embrace new challenges, often actually seeking them out. To be sure, they have problems. However, they have problems of ministry opportunity and positive momentum. Their ministry tastes flavorful and feels alive.

The differences of attitude between churched culture churches and mission outposts have a direct effect upon how they are structured. And in turn, the structure then perpetuates those attitudes.

Churched culture churches are typically **top-down** organizations. Most will even have a pyramid-type organization chart showing who has authority over whom. There are specific rules that control most decisions. While the "voters" may be asked to "approve" ideas, in reality a few people make most decisions that are then "sold" to the voters.

Mission outpost congregations have very **open** structures. Many different types of groups are empowered to develop and execute ministry activities. The mission of the congregation becomes the focus of activities.

Activities at churched culture congregations are often **dictated** by a small number of people. Sometimes this small circle includes the pastor and a few key leaders. Sometimes it is a few key leaders, excluding the pastor. It is not uncommon for a church to be controlled by one person, who may or may not be the pastor.

In many congregations the controlling party is not even a current officeholder. No decisions are made without considering the opinion of a matriarch or patriarch of the congregation, even if they are absent from the decision-making gathering.

Mission outpost congregations are highly **participative** with the membership in general making the few critical decisions. A group of leaders provides overall communication or coordination, but individuals, small task groups, or other appropriately placed ministry groups make the vast majority of major decisions.

Top-down, dictatorial structure results in an extensive amount of centralized **control** in churched culture congregations. A few people hold all the power and control everything, even relatively minor matters.

These people often lament the absence of others to take on some of the workload. Unfortunately, they really mean that they want others to do the work on activities over which they refuse to give up control. We sometimes call this "shoot yourself in the foot" leadership.

Mission outpost congregations exhibit high levels of **trust**. The leaders trust others to make effective ministry decisions within the context of the overall ministry direction determined by the congregation as a whole.

Leaders of mission outpost congregations are comfortable not knowing everything that is going on. They will often decline to approve or disapprove matters that should be determined by another individual or group.

To achieve centralized control, churched culture churches create **complex** constitution and bylaws structures. Significant amounts of time are spent dealing with relatively insignificant issues. The leaders take comfort in the certainty that they exercise authority without realizing that the control they value is the principal source of their functional difficulties.

Mission outpost congregations have a simple and **streamlined** structure. Mission, not structure, is the central theme. If the structure interferes with accomplishing some ministry, then the structure is changed.

Churched culture churches have elaborate constitutions and bylaws that are "**cast in stone**" and very difficult to change. This characteristic assures control and diminishes ministry.

Mission outpost churches develop **flexible** constitutions and bylaws that allow for easy modification of the structure as times and conditions change. This important aspect of successful Great Commission ministry requires openness and participatory leadership based upon high levels of trust.

Senior leadership meetings at churched culture churches can often be characterized as miscellaneous reports on unrelated activities. Large amounts of time are spent second-guessing decisions that could be made by a relatively small number of people in a short amount of time. Many struggling ministries are characterized as "**fully coordinated inaction**."

Mission outpost churches are much more **loosely organized**, and at the same time focused on action. This is not the random action of a churched culture congregation blindly repeating activities decade after decade. Rather, the mission outpost church is involved in activities designed to focus on achieving Great Commission ministry.

Structure

Structural differences between churched culture churches and mission outpost churches have a dramatic impact upon how they function.

Churched culture churches operate within an **institutionalized structure**. Virtually all of the boards and committees spend all their time on **issues inside** the congregation.

Volunteers are recruited from inside the current membership to participate in or run ministries. Some even go so far as to prevent nonmembers from participating in effective recruiting activities like choirs or teaching children's Sunday school.

Many of these congregations have **nominating committees** that experience great difficulty with the daunting task of finding the large numbers of people needed to fill mandated boards, committees, and activities.

The **strongest leaders in the congregation serve internally**-focused church activities. Recruiting people to fill positions in the few outreach-oriented activities that a church may have is left to the end of the recruitment effort, after the "main" positions have been filled.

An interesting analysis is to examine the amount of time the church's Lay Leadership Group spends on which issues. Churched culture churches have an institutional structure that forces their leaders to spend virtually all their **leadership time on matters within the congregation**.

In sharp contrast, the structure of mission outpost congregations changes how they function. Mission outpost congregations mostly function with mission teams rather than committees. These teams are usually smaller and are always empowered to make decisions and carry out action.

Mission teams focus outside the church on the Great Commission, even while conducting what some would consider an internal activity. Here are some examples:

- The choir in a mission outpost congregation invites nonmembers to participate. They realize that nonmember participants often bring several people with them.
- The interior design team in a mission outpost congregation pays attention to how inviting the decor is to people in the community. For example, mission outpost congregations located among people of a different culture create an environment with color schemes, furnishings, and artwork familiar to the neighbors they hope to reach with the saving message of Jesus Christ.
- The outreach team includes people from the community so that the church can stay informed about ways that it could be missionally helpful.

Mission outpost congregations spend large amounts of their **volunteer resources on activities focused on ministry outside** the congregation. They realize that spiritual growth is nourished in mission, not in meetings.

Although a small nominating committee may still exist, the primary method that mission outpost churches use to secure volunteers is through a **mobilization team**. This group helps members, regular attenders, guests, or anyone seeking to participate, to identify and use their ministry gifts. The team is not engaged in elected position "slot filling." When a ministry gift is identified that does not fit existing ministries, then either a new ministry is created or the potential volunteer is helped to find another outlet for their ministry gift, often outside the church.

While securing volunteer help is a valued component of the mobilization team's efforts, that is not its primary objective. The primary purpose of a mobilization team is nurturing spiritual growth of those who participate. Involvement in ministry is perhaps the most effective method of helping people grow spiritually.

The strongest leaders in mission outpost congregations are encouraged into the most important leadership role—**Great Commission ministry leadership**. They may accept overall leadership responsibilities for a limited amount of time. However, those stints are viewed as an interruption of their primary call—to be leading a missional ministry.

Within a mission outpost church, leadership **meeting time is spent on deciding mission strategies for the local mission field**. Within a mission outpost church, the entire structure is focused on Great Commission impact on the local mission field. While many other things happen, the thrust of the church's effort is to reach out to broken and hurting people with a healing Jesus.

Impact of Structure on Mission

All these differences between structure and function of churched culture churches versus mission outpost churches have a direct bearing upon the core functions of the congregation.

Churched culture churches are **believer-friendly**. They describe themselves as being "very friendly" places. And they are. In fact, the members are quite friendly to one another. At the same time, they are often cold to visitors and nonmembers—particularly if the outsider is not from the same denominational or heritage background.

Visitors are given no help in the location of important features like parking, restrooms, when to stand or sit, how to follow along with the order of worship, and a host of other matters. Heaven help the visitor who sits in "the wrong pew." For visitors, even the much valued "coffee time" is a cold and uninviting activity as members stand in closed groups or sit at "their table" and ignore outsiders.

Mission outpost churches are careful to help **everyone feel welcome**. They seek out ways to be inviting from the time guests enter the parking area until after they have returned home.

These churches work hard to help all members see themselves as part of the evangelism effort. Most Great Commission churches do not have evangelism committees, lest the rest of the membership think that outreach is the task of that committee or the pastor. Words that imply "we are members of this club" and "you are an outsider" are eliminated from greetings and messages. The whole atmosphere for guests is different from that of the churched culture church.

Volunteer recruitment at churched culture churches consists of **filling a large number of slots** on many boards and committees. The task is so monumental that it consumes tremendous amounts of volunteer energy simply keeping the institutional structure alive.

Mission outpost churches are focused on **spiritual growth** and development of all with whom they come in contact. Numerical growth is not the motivation. When numerical growth happens, it is a natural outcome of effective spiritual growth.

Now, please take a few minutes to examine yourself or discuss with another person: **Do these observations about how the world has changed match your experience?**

Chapter 3
The Way People Work Has Changed

Change in the culture surrounding churches today has truly affected congregations. Perhaps even more potent are changes in the way that people are willing to spend their scarcest commodity—time. The constitutions and bylaws at most congregations were developed in a time when people had different life pressures and priorities.

Sprinters and Marathoners

Ephesians 4 explains that God has blessed different people with **different gifts**. Two ways that people are different are important to matters related to church constitutions and bylaws.

Some people are excellent sprinters. On a track team, sprinters use high bursts of energy for short periods of time to accomplish goals. They are dedicated to the task and work hard for themselves and the team.

Other people are solid marathon runners. On a track team, solid marathon runners use pacing and control over long periods of time to accomplish goals. They are equally dedicated to the task and work hard for themselves and the team.

The same is true in life. Some people function best as excellent sprinters. They conduct their lives and most activities in highly creative, short-term activities. They are effective and competent in achieving goals and objectives. When going on a family vacation, sprinters are still packing as the family car backs out of the driveway.

Other people function best as solid marathon runners. They plan out and operate their lives in highly structured, long-duration activities. They are effective and competent in achieving goals and objectives. They prepare for the family va-cation by being packed several days before leaving, and rechecking their luggage several times.

Churches are mostly organized as a marathon run. Most activities take place in committees that must be joined for a term of two, three, or more years. These committees are usually required to meet regularly, whether or not they need to meet. They spend many long hours making relatively minor decisions.

When asked by the nominating committee to run for a church position, most people realize that it is not a one-term commitment of two or three years. They understand they will be renominated for a succeeding term, and, because it is getting hard to find willing candidates, one term of two or three years can stretch into what seems like a "life sentence."

The culture currently reinforces sprinter behavior. Those who have a sprinter orientation have learned to simply decline nomination to marathon activities. They choose not to invest large amounts of time participating on committees that have too many people attempting to make too few important decisions. There are so many forces competing for their time, sprinters are no longer willing to attend meetings that do not need to happen.

Two major problems are created when this difference in pacing of life comes into conflict with congregation structure as defined in the constitution and bylaws:

1. Excellent sprinters, perhaps half of all possible candidates, are automatically eliminated from participation.
2. Many solid marathon runners cannot take on another marathon activity. Thus, perhaps an additional twenty-five percent of

possible leaders are also prevented from serving.

Left Brain – Right Brain

Another difference in the orientation people have toward life is the theory of the "left brain" and "right brain." This theory stems from the neurological fact that different sides of the brain control different functions. Most people are more dominated by one side of their brain.

Consider the following differences in the ways that left and right-brained people might accomplish a task, take in information, and make decisions.

Task Focus
"The task is of primary importance in accomplishing any objective."

Relational Focus
"No, people and relationships are more important than completing a task."

Logic
"Relationships are fine, but often they are not logical. We must use good logic and sound thinking to accomplish the goal."

Emotion
"Using logic alone ignores feelings. The emotional aspects of issues need to be explored."

Facts
"Emotion can be useful, but facts are critical. The more facts we have, the better will be the decisions."

Intuition
"Facts often are not enough. Sometimes the only way to make a decision is by tapping into intuition."

Organized
"Unfortunately it is not possible to organize around intuition. We need

order to accomplish an objective. Without organization we will just go in circles, not getting anything done."

Organized differently
"There are many ways to organize, all of which can be equally effective. My desk may look disorganized to you, but I know exactly where everything is in every stack."

Pre-planned
"All that chaos makes it impossible to pre-plan every detail of all activities. It simply is not a good idea to start something unless we know exactly what will happen."

Spontaneous
"Some pre-planning is okay, but we need flexibility and openness to creativity. Spontaneity and fun will enhance any project."

Place for everything
"Spontaneous changes interrupt order. We have to stay orderly with a place for everything and everything in its place."

Whatever!!!
"Whateverrr!!!"

The churched culture existed in a predominantly left-brain dominant world. Left-brainers wrote most constitutions and bylaws. The documents contain detailed descriptions of structures and relationships. Many are so complex that they are difficult to understand and virtually impossible to follow.

During the times of the churched culture, right-brain dominant people learned to accommodate themselves to the left-brain world in order to participate.

Congregation leaders automatically prevent large numbers of potential leaders and workers from serving because they ignore the contribution of people who think differently. Nominating committees largely ignore creative and talented people because they "think differently." Many creative people decline to participate with closed-minded people who only know one way of doing things.

God's mission needs both sides of the brain. Mission outpost churches eagerly embrace all the gifts God has graciously given them. They intentionally match people into ministries according to their gifts and passions.

How are you oriented on these two dimensions? By yourself or with another person, examine your preferences and how those styles of functioning affect your involvement in God's mission. **Are you predominantly left or right-brained? Are you mostly an excellent sprinter or a solid marathon runner?**

Sprinter Approaches

Kennon Callahan has pointed out several ways in which sprinter approaches help churches achieve Great Commission ministry. For example, many church leaders use the phrase "what we need is for people to **work harder** and be more committed" as they lament the difficulty of finding others to share the load.

It is more helpful to **work smarter** than to work harder. This means creating new ways to deal with challenges. These are ways that more closely match the realities of the unchurched culture.

The first of two fundamental ways of working smarter not harder is to **plan less to achieve more**. This means spending the right amount of time in planning—far less time than what currently happens in most churches. Timely decisions are made by the appropriate individual or group. Congregations are action-oriented, not bogged down in procedures.

The second fundamental way to work smarter not harder is to recognize that **progress is more helpful than perfection**. Making progress and getting to the action is severely impeded in many churches by a desire to be sure everything is perfectly planned before an activity can proceed. Over-planning delays action, saps energy, discourages eager volunteers, and drives away the needed workers and leaders that many congregations desire.

Passion for excellence is different from compulsive obsession for perfection. Excellence is always a desired factor. A compulsion to achieve perfection is not the same thing as a desire for excellence. Perfectionism kills ideas and drives away new helpers and leaders. Perfectionism is a disease that kills the perfectionist and everyone around. The goal is to achieve excellence by empowering people to use their God-given gifts.

That simple goal is at the heart of the effort to create a flexible, missional constitution and bylaws using the methods described in this book.

Chapter 4
Structuring Congregations Has Changed

Changing from a churched to an unchurched culture has had a profound effect upon how congregations can operate. The changes in what people will and will no longer tolerate have had an equally powerful impact upon how churches are structured.

These two types of changes in the environment are challenging the way congregations have traditionally functioned. Most congregations are responding to volunteer and leadership shortages with traditional solutions. These solutions are generally characterized as "people just need to work harder" or "people need more commitment." The changes described in the two previous chapters clearly show that the normally applied "solutions" simply make the problem worse.

Fortunately, congregations are no longer at the mercy of these upheavals. Solutions have already been found, tested, and demonstrated to work. Moreover, congregations that adopt a different philosophy of leadership find that those who participate with the congregation are also experiencing increased levels of spiritual growth.

The leadership model found to be effective in current times is articulated well in three books. One is John Carver's book *Boards That Make a Difference* (ISBN 1-55542-231-4). The other two are Kennon Callahan's *Twelve Keys to an Effective Church* (ISBN 0-7879-3871-8) and *Effective Church Leadership* (ISBN 0-7879-3865-3).

The structure explained in this chapter applies the principles laid out by Carver and Callahan. When joined with the concepts described in the prior chapters, these ideas create the basis for a constitution and bylaws that are flexible and missional.

Before exploring the structural issues, we need to explain one important understanding about the nature of congregational decisions. In his books, Kennon Callahan describes "**The 20-80 Principle**."

Most church members are familiar with the term "20-80." They hear it expressed as "twenty percent of the people do eighty percent of the work" or "twenty percent of the people give eighty percent of the money." Callahan uses the phrase in a different way.

He suggests that within congregational decision-making, twenty percent of all decisions generate eighty percent of the ministry results. Conversely, eighty percent of the decisions made by a congregation create only twenty percent of the ministry results. He encourages church leaders to focus on twenty-percenter decisions, and delegate eighty-percenter decisions to one or two empowered people.

Some examples of the questions that generate twenty-percenter decisions are:

1. Shall the primary mission of this congregation be ministry to children and their families?
2. If the primary ministry is to children and their families, shall we create a nursery and pre-school?
3. Because we previously decided to be a mission outpost to the different types of people in our local mission field, shall we offer more than one type of worship service each week?
4. Who is God calling us to serve? What are their human hurts and hopes?
5. What shall be the mission and structure of our congregation?
6. What are our gifts, strengths, and competencies?

Most congregations struggling with leadership and volunteer issues spend the vast majority of the senior leadership time grappling with eighty-percenter decisions. While these decisions do need to be made, Callahan helpfully points out that none of these decisions has a major impact on the overall ministry experience of the church. He also suggests that one or two persons make these decisions, not requiring any time by the Lay Leadership Group or pastor.

Some examples of the questions that lead to eighty-percenter decisions are:

1. Shall we spend three hundred dollars on a new photocopier?
2. Shall we accept the donation of an artificial Christmas tree?
3. What color will we paint the walls of the bathrooms?
4. Should the ushers have badges with their names printed on them, should they be allowed to take them home, should there be a fine if they fail to bring them back for worship services, how much should the fine be, and what will we do with the accumulated fine money?

Both Callahan and Carver point to the same two-pronged primary leadership and decision-making principle. It is that the congregation and key leaders should make twenty-percenter decisions and that they should make only twenty-percenter decisions.

In most churches the senior decision-making body is some form of a Voters' Assembly. This group is often referred to as "the congregation" or "the members." In some congregations this group is almost everyone who participates, and in other congregations it is a much smaller portion.

Voters' Assembly

The Voters should make many of the **twenty-percenter decisions**. More importantly, the Voters only make decisions that are at the twenty-percenter level. For example:

1. The Voters determine the overall **direction of the ministry**. The central focus of the ministry is not left to chance, habit, or platitudes. It is articulated in a specific fashion.

2. The Voters decide the specific **outcomes** intended to achieve that direction. They determine the level of accomplishment that is desired and to which they are committed.

This is a new notion for most churches. They have a habit of simply conducting a large number of activities with no thought as to whether or not those activities are accomplishing the desired overall outcome.

Establishing ministry outcomes is a critical element of accomplishing the overall ministry goal. Without outcomes, churches have no way of knowing the value of specific activities.

3. The Voters define how those outcomes will be approached when they **approve the ministry plan**, often presented in the form of the annual budget. However, a key difference from current practice is that the budget is displayed in ministry areas such as local outreach, youth programs, children's ministries, and so forth. The staff and overhead costs of those activities are included within the ministry budget, and not lumped into a line item called "personnel."

4. The Voters make the major staff decisions, especially those sometimes referred to as "**divine call**." Selection of individuals to key positions is critical to accomplishment of the congregation's mission.

Rescinding a divine call is a sensitive issue. Some denominational polity dictates that divine calls can never be rescinded. Other denominations feel that firing a called worker can happen at the will of the congregation or a denominational official. Most traditions allow for termination of a person with a divine call under prescribed conditions. In all cases, it is the Voters who should make that decision.

5. The Voters make the **major program decisions**, such as whether or not to operate a pre-school. These major program decisions further define the ministry of the congregation. They also represent substantial commitments of volunteer and financial resources.

6. The Voters make major decisions about **acquiring or selling real estate, property**, or other large dollar amount items. Conversely, Voters are never involved in relatively minor financial decisions. The helpful rule of thumb is to keep decisions of less than some percentage of the budget (e.g. 10% of budgeted expenses) off the agenda of Voters' meetings.

7. The Voters **elect the officers and the "Lay Leadership Group."** These leaders are charged with the responsibility of carrying out the directions and plans adopted by the congregation.

   The important point to keep in mind is that the Voters always retain authority to define and redefine the focus of the congregation's ministry. They also retain the authority to select and "unselect" the key paid and volunteer individuals who carry out the wishes of the Voters.

8. One final point about the Voters is critical. This point is also a major difference between a missional constitution and most of the current structural approaches of congregations.

   The Voters **make no decisions about operational details**. They are never asked to deal with eighty-percenter issues. This approach honors the reality that time is the most precious commodity possessed by people. Voters are eager to invest in meaningful use of their time, and will not expend their time in minor decisions that could easily be made by one or two people.

Each of the listed major decisions determines the direction and nature of the church's ministry. The entire congregation makes these decisions. That does not mean the congregation approves the recommendations brought to it by a board or committee. It means the congregation grapples with the central issues and makes the decisions.

The term "entire congregation" means twenty to forty percent of average weekly worship attendance. For most churches, this will be a huge increase over current attendance at Voters' meetings.

Some react to this percentage by saying that this large a group cannot assess and make decisions. This simply is not the case. In fact, this book shows how a large number of people can redraft the constitution and bylaws.

Some point out that this many people do not attend Voters' meetings now. The reason only a few people participate in Voters' meetings is because most meeting time is spent on eighty-percenter decisions. If a twenty-percenter decision is needed, that decision has already been made by a small group of people. The Voters' meeting is simply a "selling" process that asks the Voters to "rubber stamp" a decision that has already been made.

An example is the typical approach to creating a long-range plan. A small committee works for one or two years to create a plan. Sometimes they ask members for input, but the committee creates the plan. When completed, the plan is "sold" to the Lay Leadership Group, and then "sold" to the Voters. The Voters approve the plan and the leaders mistakenly think the congregation is "behind the plan." Most such plans then sit on a shelf gathering dust for five or ten years until the next long-range planning committee is assembled and the same failed process is repeated.

Congregation leaders wonder what happened. After all, the Voters approved the plan. No, the Voters really said, "We don't violently object. You go ahead if you want, but we do not plan to actively participate in something we did not shape." This common approach to planning was developed during the days of the churched culture and no longer works.

People are eager to attend meetings at which twenty-percenter issues are grappled with and important decisions are made.

One final factor about twenty-percenter decisions is that because they are major, it is not necessary to make very many each year. In fact, other than in times of crisis, holding monthly or quarterly Voters' meetings is typically a signal that eighty-percenter issues are being raised.

Lay Leadership Group

The next level of structure within a missional constitution and bylaws can have many different labels. For our purposes, the term "Lay Leadership Group" is used. In most churches it consists of the elected officers, program leaders, members-at-large, and representation from the staff. Churches use terms like Vestry, Session, Church Council, Board of Directors, and Parish Planning Council.

The Lay Leadership Group in the flexible, missional approach has four common characteristics. First, it is **elected at large** from the membership. Being the leader from one of the various boards and committees does not provide membership on the Group.

Second, the people on the Lay Leadership Group are there to **represent the congregation as a whole**. They are charged with making decisions for the good of the whole church. They are not there to represent, speak for, or see that the interests of any specific group are preserved.

Third, their primary **responsibility is achievement of the mission and overall outcomes** selected by the congregation. They are not there to impose their will upon the congregation.

Fourth, they do not oversee the day-to-day operations of the church. As such, the Lay Leadership Group is **not responsible for any program** of the church. In fact, except in the smallest congregations, these individuals are often precluded from leading any board, committee, or action team that reports to the Lay Leadership Group.

Although many different **names** can be used, it is most helpful if the Lay Leadership Group's name carries a connotation of representing the whole, rather than parts within the whole. Terms like **board of directors, vestry, session, or mission council** can be used when the connotation is representing the whole congregation.

Historically, the Lay Leadership Group in some traditions is a gathering of the leaders of the major church boards. That concept is not helpful in the flexible, missional approach. The council generally spends its meetings listening to **miscellaneous reports of unrelated activities that are focused mostly on needs within the church**. The very nature of the group virtually guarantees they will spend their time on eighty-percenters. The result is a large amount of activity, but with the whole congregation achieving relatively little ministry.

This approach creates an interesting phenomenon. **When everyone is responsible for the mission, nobody is responsible for the mission**.

Most current leadership groups work on the assumption that if everyone is busy, the mission of the congregation is being achieved. That notion was central to church structure in the days of the churched culture. On a mission field, intentional and focused action that produces outcomes is required. Thus, the duties of the Lay Leadership Group are focused on the whole, rather than the individual parts of the church.

Some traditions currently have Lay Leadership Groups that purport to have an overall mission focus. However, examination of their meeting minutes reveals a preponderance of internal, operational decisions, and very little discussion of overall ministry accomplishment.

In other traditions, the following duties of the Lay Leadership Group will be a major departure from what is familiar. The good news is that hundreds of congregations have already adopted this approach. They have found it to be both beneficial to the congregation and more satisfying for the individuals involved.

The Lay Leadership Group has several primary duties:

1. First, they are **empowered to create the structure needed to accomplish the mission**. This means creating boards, committees, task forces, action teams, or whatever will most effectively accomplish the activity using the resources that God has provided.

2. It is **empowered to change the structure** as conditions or resources change. These first two characteristics are at the heart of the flexibility provided in this approach. It is no longer necessary to amend the con-

stitution or bylaws when a change of structure is needed.

If the Lay Leadership Group violates its responsibility, the Voters simply vote them out of office. The congregation remains in charge.

3. Third, accompanying the authority to create and recreate structure is the responsibility for **developing and changing policies needed to achieve the overall plan and specific outcomes**. These policies ensure coordination. More importantly, they are constructed to keep the focus on how individual efforts contribute to the ministry accomplishment of the church as a whole.

Here again, it is important to be clear that the Voters define the plans and outcomes. As such, the Voters retain authority and vote the individuals out of office who choose to attempt to impose their personal will on the larger group.

4. The Lay Leadership Group is **responsible for seeing that the annual mission plan of the congregation is implemented**. This annual mission plan is usually articulated in the form of an annual budget.

For some people, it is helpful at this point to again emphasize that the congregation has determined the ministry plan. The Lay Leadership Group is charged with the responsibility for caring out that plan. If they go off in a direction different from the one the congregation has selected, they are not re-elected.

5. A major responsibility of the Lay Leadership Group is to assure the **overall fit of the various ministries and activities** of the congregation. They are aware of all the major aspects of the activities being conducted in the name of the church. From that vantage point they can see if the individual areas of the congregation's work plan are likely to add up to the accomplishment of the congregation's whole mission. Because they focus on the mission of the church as a whole, they are able to see weaknesses or oversights that need to be addressed.

6. As a general rule, the Lay Leadership Group **stays out of all administrative details**. They are not there to oversee the day-to-day operations of the church, its employees, or its volunteers.

Avoiding details provides the time needed to focus on the overall ministry. Conversely, when this group allows itself to consider eighty-percenter issues, it assures itself of long meetings dealing with trivial matters such that many of its best potential leaders will decide they do not have the time to serve on this group. Large numbers of people today no longer have the time, patience, or desire to deal with matters in large groups that can be effectively handled by individuals.

7. An important principle of leadership is that individuals and groups need to be accountable to only one other entity. That means that the Lay Leadership Group **supervises the Senior Pastor**.

In some traditions the pastor is accountable to the Lay Leadership Group in all matters. In some traditions this responsibility is for temporal matters, with spiritual oversight resting within the denomination's ecclesiastical hierarchy or directly with God in heaven.

Still other denominations have a tradition of the pastor being answerable to the church council for some things, the elders for some things, and a handful of long-term members for everything. The primary outcome of this arrangement is depression, despair, and burnout in large numbers of parish pastors and their families. It also holds the congregation hostage to the wishes of a few strong-willed people. This approach is generally destructive and almost always ministry-limiting.

8. Basically, the Lay Leadership Group has **full authority to act**, except for those few matters retained by the Voters. This is an important principle of flexible, missional church structures. Expecting leaders to have responsibility without authority to carry out that responsibility generally re-

sults in two negative outcomes. First, leaders become frustrated and give up. Second, potential leaders decline to participate in leadership.

Some are very concerned about the notion of one group having too much power. This is a common characteristic of churches that are stuck in the churched culture. People in these churches have low levels of trust for one another. Mostly these congregations are struggling.

People within thriving ministries exhibit high trust for each other. They are gospel-centered such that differences of opinion are handled in appropriate ways. When the members focus on the mission, relatively minor issues are not allowed to interfere.

Constitutions and bylaws that are missional and flexible generally use the following wording. **"The Lay Leadership Group may not**

- **issue a divine call**

- **sell or acquire real estate**

- **incur annual non-budget expenses exceeding 10% of the annual budget**

- **operate without an Annual Financial Plan approved by the Voters**

- **dissolve the congregation"**

Within this wording, the Voters retain for themselves significant matters. Some congregations will add or delete from this general list.

There are two important points. First, the Voters remain in control of the major twenty-percenters. Second, the Voters convey to the Lay Leadership Group the authority that is needed to accomplish the mission and ministry defined by the Voters.

Senior Pastor

Some congregations have several clergy, some have one full-time pastor, some share clergy with other churches, some have one part-time pastor, and some receive pastoral coverage in other ways. In virtually all churches there is someone who oversees the ministry (unless temporarily vacant).

In virtually all congregations, the Senior Pastor is **the spiritual leader of the church**. Ul-timate responsibility lies with this individual for the spiritual welfare of the members. Sometimes this individual makes theological decisions about individuals or the ministry. In churches affiliated with denominations, this person is usually linked in some way to the ecclesiastical hierarchy of the denomination.

The philosophy and practice of a flexible, missional constitution and bylaws makes no change in this common arrangement.

Sometimes the suggested approach creates situations that cause the Senior Pastor to become more clear about the differences between spiritual and temporal matters. Some pastors trained and experienced in the ways of the churched culture are firmly entrenched in the notion that they must be well aware of or even have ultimate control over all things happening at the church. These clergy tend to have difficulty adjusting to the requirements of a flexible, missional constitution and bylaws.

Prior sections made the clear statement that the congregation as a whole determines the **ministry direction of the church**. That statement takes nothing away from the central role of the Senior Pastor in decisions about the church's direction. There is no doubt that the pastor has a major influence on the congregation's understanding of its central role and function.

As pastors preach and teach, they communicate values of faith and specifics of ministry. As they exercise leadership, they influence the leadership practice of others. Kennon Callahan is very clear that people lead in direct relation to the ways they experience being led.

Generally the Senior Pastor is the **administrative leader of the church**. This is particularly true when the pastor also has personal gifts and skills for those activities.

But that is not always the case. In fact, although often desirable, it is not a requirement that the pastor eagerly adopt the role of administrative leader.

One of the key strengths of this model is the flexibility it affords the congregation to adopt a structure that best fits the gifts with which God has blessed it. If one Senior Pastor has administrative gifts, the structure can be modified by the

Lay Leadership Group to assign those activities to that gifted individual. If another Senior Pastor is less gifted in administration, then the Lay Leadership Group is authorized to make the necessary adjustments without requiring amendments to the constitution or bylaws.

In most situations, the Senior Pastor has four primary responsibilities for the temporal matters of the congregation. This list of activities can be modified by the Lay Leadership Group as necessary to best utilize the gifts of the pastor and others.

1. The first responsibility is to **implement all policies and programs** defined by the congregation and the Lay Leadership Group. The pastor has authority to adopt the means and methods needed to make that happen, within the framework of the direction set by the Voters.

   When engaged in activities as pastor of the church, the pastor is prohibited from unilaterally starting or operating a ministry that is outside the ministry defined by the congregation. Pastors choosing to conduct such ministries "on their own time" should be very careful about the confusion that type of arrangement can easily cause.

2. The Senior Pastor is authorized to **create the infrastructure necessary** to accomplish the congregation's self-selected mission and ministry.

   For example, within the context of the annual ministry plan (annual budget) the pastor is authorized to employ or terminate employment of paid or volunteer personnel. These matters are not part of the domain of the Lay Leadership Group or the Voters. The reason for this authority is clear. An individual cannot be held accountable for ministry outcomes without authority to create or modify the means of achieving those outcomes.

3. **All paid and volunteer staff are accountable only to the Senior Pastor or someone delegated by the pastor.** This administrative structure makes it clear who is authorized to make work assignments or evaluate work activities.

This characteristic exists to assure that all are working together and toward the same ends. It is designed to prevent conflicting ministry preferences from defeating the overall ministry of the church.

There are two important components of this principle that bear emphasis. First, as Carver so clearly explains, no individual on the Lay Leadership Group is authorized to give work assignments to staff or volunteers. This characteristic protects workers from interference by individuals with a particular interest that is not in concert with the ministry selected by the congregation or pursuing a path of action that varies from the approach being followed by the ministry as a whole.

The second component is also a key element of the Carver model. Every person or group is only answerable to one individual or group. This characteristic is essential to avoid conflict about methods and procedures catching people "in the middle" between conflicted individuals.

Sometimes a congregation will choose to have a key employee, like a school principal or major program administrator, report directly to the Lay Leadership Group rather than to the Senior Pastor. This arrangement is highly risky and strongly discouraged.

4. The Senior Pastor is granted **authority for emergency spending up to some percentage (perhaps five percent) of the budget.** The annual ministry plan (annual budget) provides sufficient financial resources to operate the ministry. Keeping spending within the budget is aided by the more common situation that income lags behind projections, and extra funds simply are not available.

   Sometimes a special situation can arise in which expenditures need to be made that are outside the ministry plan. As a general principle, the Senior Pastor is well advised to discuss such matters with the Lay Leadership Group prior to taking action. The model recognizes that sometimes advance discussion is not possible and suggests that the Senior Pastor be given authority to unilaterally spend up to some amount, usually expressed as a percentage of the annual budget.

As with the Lay Leadership Group, the wording of constitutions and bylaws that are flexible and missional generally stipulates that the **Senior Leadership Pastor may not:**

- **discharge a called worker**
- **create a new ministry program**
- **incur annual non-budget expenses exceeding 5% of the annual budget**

Some congregations add a few additional items to this list. The overarching principle is that the Senior Pastor has full authority to take action except where specifically prohibited. Those matters are reserved to the Lay Leadership Group or the Voters.

Action Teams

As previously explained, the current culture is more sprinter than marathon runner oriented. Churches have a habit of defining activities with a marathon runner approach. As a result, large numbers of people in the current culture are automatically eliminated from ministry or leadership because they are unwilling or simply unable to devote large amounts of time over an extended number of months or years to participate.

Mission outpost churches having difficulty securing needed volunteers to support activities usually have those problems because the activity is structured as a marathon. The churches will generally deal with the problem by adopting one of two solutions. Either they will divide the activity into a number of smaller and shorter tasks, or they will no longer conduct the activity.

In a flexible, missional constitution and bylaws, much of the work is conducted with task forces or **action teams**.

Action teams **meet only when they need to meet**. Some, like a properties group, will meet regularly year round. Others, like the Vacation Bible School team, will only meet intensively for a few months every spring and then rest for the remainder of the year. Still others, like the

lounge remodeling team, will meet frequently until the project is done, celebrate completion of the project, and then disband. Action teams meet when there is work to be done and do not waste time by gathering unnecessarily.

Membership on action teams consists of those who have competence in the activity to be completed. In the churched culture, it was common for people to participate on committees for which they had no background and limited interest. They served out of duty and commitment.

The problem with this approach is that marginally interested people with limited background or competence produce marginally effective activities that yield limited results.

In most cases it is better to discontinue an activity if competent people cannot be found. Many church leaders object to this notion, arguing that the activity is important and must go on the way it has in the past. They contend that people simply must be found to accept the responsibility.

Our response is threefold:
1. Many activities do not have to continue.
2. Those that do could be done in a different way.
3. If done in a different way, there are almost always interested volunteers available when churches stop operating as a marathon runner activity and start helping people see ministry as a spiritual growth opportunity.

Action teams should be the correct size. Normally that means they should be **relatively small**. This way, the ministry will not become bogged down by the constant need to negotiate compromise on hundreds of relatively minor issues. Also, the time commitment of team members is respected by reducing the number of opinions that must be considered on minor matters.

Many congregations have term limits of two, three, or four years for membership on existing boards and committees. The result is that at just about the time team members begin to understand their task, they are rotated out of office. This concept virtually guarantees mediocre programs that simply repeat what was done in past years.

Another approach is to permit people to belong to an action team for **as long as they have interest and the team is achieving its goals**. Sometimes congregation leaders object to this notion, citing concerns about centralization of power or perpetuation of incompetence. Those two problems do not happen, but for reasons that will be explained later.

Standing Boards and Committees

Some congregations will retain a **few standing boards or committees**. They can be elected, but most are better operated if appointed or self-selected. For example, it is more helpful to appoint people with competence in the techniques and procedures of human resources to a Personnel Committee. A different example might be a Properties Committee made up of anyone interested in helping.

Standing committees should be the **right size** needed for the task rather than automatically being a large group. Large committees are usually intended to ensure representation. The reality is that large committees virtually guarantee inaction.

As with action teams, congregations will be better served when continuity is coupled with competence. **Removing term limits** is helpful in securing those two valuable assets.

Teams, boards and committees

A congregation that has a flexible, missional constitution and bylaws eagerly permits the Lay Leadership Group to create an **assortment of action teams, task forces, boards, standing committees, temporary committees**, and any other group appropriate to the task at hand. The members of the congregation find a wide variety of ways they can use their gifts from God in a manner more appropriate to the realities of their lives.

The overall ministry of the congregation proceeds in a **coordinated manner as created and updated by the Lay Leadership Group.**

Most groups consist **of individuals gifted by God** who have a longing to be helpful in a particular ministry. Some teams or boards require specific content expertise in addition to a desire to be helpful (e.g. financial investment, money management, legal issues, etc.).

Within the context of the congregation's overall ministry and the general principles defined by the Lay Leadership Group, each board, committee, or team **defines its own structure and function**. Those in the best position to know how to organize and approach the work are empowered to conduct their ministries.

Some of these teams, boards, and committees have a primary purpose of **consultation, and others exist to implement** ministry. An example of a consultative team is the Youth Council in churches that have a Director of Youth Ministry.

Because an individual is accountable to only one entity, the Youth Director reports to and receives work assignments from the Senior Pastor, not the Youth Council. The Youth Council is a valuable asset of the youth program, provides input to the planning, and supports the Youth Director in a wide variety of ways. But the Youth Council does not give work instructions to the Youth Director.

In a different congregation, there may not be a Director of Youth Ministry. In that situation, the Youth Council becomes responsible for implementing the youth programs and is accountable to the Lay Leadership Group or the Senior Pastor.

The principles underlying the structure of congregations in current times have changed from what worked in prior days. The current constitution and bylaws in most churches were developed during the days of the churched culture. Different times require different methods.

Fortunately, many congregations have already pioneered these methods. They have learned, sometimes with difficulty, what works and what does not. While these structural insights may seem new, they are not. They have been studied, tested, and found to be effective.

Chapter 5
Creating the Event

Basically, there are two methods available to churches wishing to consider changing their constitution and bylaws. One is to create a Constitution Study Committee. That group might collect sample constitutions from a variety of churches for comparison with their current document. Study sessions could be held. The group could read leadership and organizational books, usually including the Carver and Callahan books referenced in Chapter 4.

The typical Constitution Study Committee takes a year or two (sometimes longer) to assess the options and generate a draft. The draft is reviewed, discussed, and reworked by the Lay Leadership Group. It is then presented to the Voters for more review, discussion, and rewriting. The entire process can easily stretch beyond two years.

The option described in this book involves about three months to organize an event that creates a draft constitution and bylaws on one Saturday.

Chapter 5 is a step-by-step guide to organizing the one-day event in which a facilitator helps the entire congregation rewrite the constitution and bylaws. At the end of that one-day event, the church will have a document that is ninety to ninety-nine percent complete.

One-Day Event

This is a one-day event. By that we mean a Saturday from about 8:30 a.m. until 4:30 p.m. We encourage a Saturday, even if there is to be worship on Saturday evening. The Saturday evening service can be used to celebrate all that was accomplished on that day for the mission of Christ.

We discourage attempting this event in one day on a Sunday, especially if Sunday morning is the primary time for worship and Bible study. That would be a very long day, requiring two meals, extended child care, and a host of other complications.

The notion of doing it all in one day comes from two primary motivations:
1. Only one day is needed.
2. Spreading the event over several days splits the continuity of the content and reduces momentum.

Example Agenda

8:00	Registration, coffee, fruit, donuts Child care opens
8:30	Opening devotion
8:40	Thank organizers Introduce facilitator
8:45	Present content in Chapters 2 and 3
9:30	Presentation about issues with the current constitution and bylaws
9:45	Present content in Chapter 4
10:30	Break (can precede Chapter 4)
11:00	Chapter 6 – Constitution
Noon	Lunch
1:00	Reconvene for directions (Chapter 7)
1:10	Bylaws subgroups meet
2:30	Break
3:00	Bringing constitution and bylaws together (Chapter 8)

4:25 Closing prayer

4:30 Adjourn

The specific starting time is determined by what is common in the local community. Some communities prefer to start at 8:00 a.m. and others would not dare begin before 9:00 a.m.

The announced ending time should take the following points into consideration:

1. Do not announce an ending time that allows for less that the time frame suggested above. More time is generally not needed, but scheduling less time can create substantial problems.

2. Allow thirty minutes for each of the two breaks or a full sixty minutes for lunch. This is an intense meeting. In order to stay fresh and focused, the participants will need that time to relax.

3. It is better to announce a later ending time and then adjourn early than to have to ask people to stay longer.

4. People will devote this amount of time to an event of this significance. In some ways, the amount of time being asked helps to reinforce the event's importance.

If the event cannot be completed in one day, then either of the following two approaches can be used:

Two four-hour time slots
1. Chapters 2 – 4
2. Chapters 6 – 8

Three three-hour time slots
1. Chapters 2 – 4
2. Chapters 6 – 7
3. Chapter 8

Facilitator

The facilitator must be skilled at leading complex meetings. We urge congregations to use a facilitator from outside the church. The dynamics of this process require that the person leading the meeting not be perceived as having any personal agenda.

The facilitator's only responsibility is to the process and to keeping the process moving. Sometimes the facilitator also presents the information in Chapters 2, 3, and 4. Other churches ask one, two, or three others to make those presentations.

If the facilitator comes from within the congregation, that individual must be widely regarded as impartial and objective to the issues being discussed.

The congregation's Pastor(s) should never facilitate the event. Pastor(s) have key functions as spiritual leaders, supportive persons, and resources.

Sometimes the congregation's judicatory (e.g. district, synod, presbytery, conference, convention, etc.) will have staff available. Most of these individuals can be objective and would be viewed as such by the participants. However, that is not automatic.

The facilitator must be committed to helping the assembly create a document that makes best sense for the congregation, even if some of the choices are different from the facilitator's personal preferences. Be sure to ask the facilitator to explain how they would handle any differences between their preferences and the choices made by the congregation.

This event is more complex than can be handled by someone new to the art of facilitating large meetings. While this book provides an explanation of procedures that will work in most churches, once in a while a situation develops that calls for a major adjustment. The facilitator should be sufficiently skilled to make adjustments and keep the process moving.

Selection of the facilitator requires care. Some congregations choose an internal person or judicatory representative primarily because they will not charge a fee. That can work. It is also true that the "low cost" route can prove to be very expensive in the long run.

The body of this document contains a large number of notes to the facilitator appropriate to what is happening in the event at that time. Appendix F provides additional notes for the facilitator.

Entire Congregation

The event is intended to include the entire congregation. This means twenty to forty percent of the average weekly worship attendance. Congregations with smaller average worship attendance are encouraged to be on the high end of this range. The more who attend, the better will be the results.

Three advantages accrue to having large attendance:

1. Everyone has the same information. These are not "closed meetings" that are perceived to be a few people telling the rest what to do. Openness creates trust. Trust creates comfort. Comfort creates approval.

2. When attendance is larger than typical Voters' meeting participation, approval becomes assured.

3. Some congregations must deal with a few people who insist on getting their own way. Large attendance effectively blunts the influence of those who might like to hold the majority hostage to the points of view held by themselves and their small circle of friends.

Rewrite Constitution and Bylaws

This event leads the members through a series of decisions needed to create a flexible, missional constitution and bylaws. Sample wording is provided so participants can discuss specifics.

The gathering does not "wordsmith" the specific text. It provides enough direction that one individual can finish the text needed for submission to the current constitution's change procedures.

Our experience is that at the end of the day, virtually all of the major decisions will have been made. Once in a while, there are one or two items that the members do not feel prepared to decide. However, this is much rarer than might be expected. Chapter 8 provides a specific procedure to determine if any issue truly is something needing further consideration. Mostly, these issues have a very small number of people who simply do not understand or will not accept that their point of view is a clear minority.

Chapter 9 explains how to complete the document draft and proceed to adoption and implementation.

Preparation

Preparation for the event is straightforward. The principal steps are:

1. **Investigate options.** The congregation's key leaders normally are the most motivated to simplify the constitution and bylaws. They are the ones most affected by the problems. Sometimes the entire Lay Leadership Group interviews consultants or reads books and other materials. Sometimes officials from the judicatory are consulted. The church's key leaders may wish to read, discuss, and assess this book.

2. **Selecting a course of action.** The approach defined in this book closely matches the key characteristics of flexible, missional constitutions. The book explains how to use the right amount of time to make excellent decisions—in this case, one day.

3. **Appoint a steering team.** A group of four to seven people completes all the arrangements needed for a successful event. The steering team is not asked to develop a draft constitution and bylaws. The entire congregation does the drafting during the event this steering team creates.

4. **Secure facilitator.** The event will need an individual to facilitate the discussion. This person must be viewed by those attending the event as unbiased. The facilitator must have experience at leading large groups in general discussion. Ability to deal with individuals possessing strong opinions is required. Most important is the facilitator's commitment to the whole group making decisions for itself. This event is no place for a beginner facilitator.

Under no circumstances should the pastor or any paid staff member be the facilitator. It is best if the facilitator comes from outside the congregation. It is helpful if the facilitator is familiar with the language and structure of church constitutions.

5. **Select a date.** Picking the date for the event can be a challenge. The most important factor is the availability of the largest possible number of people. In most congregations this means the largest number of members.

In some congregations those who can vote are a very small portion of the membership or frequent attenders. These churches have to make a fundamental decision about who is invited to the event. We encourage the leaders to set aside the current constitutional prescription and consider, "Who do we want to participate in leadership?" Remember that this is a drafting process. Final adoption occurs later and must follow the procedures stated in the existing constitution or bylaws.

Select a date that will allow at least two full months for promotion. Three or four months of lead time are more helpful.

Above all, resist the temptation to pick an early or poorly-timed date to get the problem "fixed" in a hurry. Never hold the event between mid-November and New Year's Day. Be careful about late June to mid-August. Always avoid the Super Bowl weekend or major community events.

6. **Select a site.** The location requires two types of rooms. A main room needs to be large enough to hold the entire group. While seating around tables is best, rows of chairs (theater style) will also work. Comfortable chairs and good lighting are important. The sanctuary should generally not be used unless it already serves as a multi-purpose room.

The main room needs to be made dark enough for the projection of printed text (described in the "Technology" section below). If the room cannot be darkened, then the projector must be brighter.

The location also needs at least five separate meeting rooms, each capable of holding twenty percent of the expected attendance. These are used by subgroups in the afternoon as attendees consider the content of the bylaws. It is best if the main room is not used by any of the subgroups.

It is impossible for the subgroups to meet in "corners" of the main room. There will be too much noise for the subgroups to function effectively.

7. **Pick a theme.** A theme will spark interest and encourage participation. An invitational theme is more helpful than a commanding theme. Avoid words like "duty," "task," or "responsibility."

Some on the event steering team or the congregation's leadership may have to honestly admit that creating themes is not their best skill. If the leadership group has nobody gifted at this critical activity, they have an opportunity to give others a chance for meaningful participation by asking them to come up with the theme. Some examples of themes used by congregations we have facilitated are:

- "Pioneering the New Millennium" – a Colorado congregation
- "A Rainbow of Mission" – a Hawaiian theme in Duluth in January
- "<u>F</u>ully <u>R</u>elying <u>O</u>n <u>G</u>od" – a church located in a neighborhood proudly known as FROGtown

8. **Focus on attendance**. Attendance by large numbers is critical to making good decisions. When large numbers attend the event, approval becomes virtually automatic.

The steering team focuses a major portion of its efforts on encouraging attendance. The date, theme, location, and event promotion are critical components of achieving attendance by a high percentage of those eligible to attend.

We strongly encourage that the young people of the congregation be actively recruited. We are always amazed at how many congregations complain about youth and young adults not being involved, but at the same time do not permit young people to participate in discussing significant issues.

ote, **Promote, Promote.** Promoting the event must start at least two months prior to the event. Three or four months ahead of time is better. People will want to attend the event, but must get it onto their personal calendars soon enough that other commitments do not prevent attendance.

Promotion is aided by remembering that not everyone reads the church's monthly newsletter or weekly worship bulletin announcements. Many congregations decide this event is so important that they send personal invitations to everyone. Most congregations find that regular reminders from the pastor(s) at worship, meetings, and other activities help people understand that this is an important event. Personal, verbal invitations are the most effective.

Promotion announcements, whether verbal, printed, or electronic, should have a spirit of invitation and excitement. Avoid words that communicate duty or responsibility.

10. **Child care.** Someone with expertise should arrange child care. Child care has many aspects that an enthused person without experience will not know.

If at all possible, ask people who are not eligible to participate in the event to provide child care. When members or young people of the congregation are asked to staff the child care, they are excluded from an important event in the life of the church. It may be better to hire staff from a local preschool to operate the child care so that all members can participate in the event.

11. **Food.** The agenda indicates several food-related needs. Think of it as hosting an all-day family reunion. Coffee, juice, fruit, breads, and pastries are welcoming arrival refreshments before the event starts. A midmorning break can repeat the arrival menu.

Lunch should be capable of being served and cleaned up in forty-five minutes. Sometimes that means box lunches.

Serving a hot meal to a large gathering means more than one serving line.

Many congregations have the lunch catered. They want to give everyone an opportunity to participate, rather than losing a large number of people to the task of food preparation.

12. **Handouts.** The assembly will need a number of handouts. These materials already exist. Preparation is merely a matter of gathering the documents, reproducing, and distributing them. Handouts for everyone as they arrive are:

- A time schedule for the day
- The current constitution and bylaws (yes, the whole document, especially if it is thirty or more pages)
- The Constitution and Bylaws of St. Paul Church printed in Appendix A

Handouts for the afternoon subgroup sessions should be gathered within the subgroupings described in Chapter 7. Prepare enough copies for thirty percent of the total expected attendance. For example, if one hundred people are expected, then reproduce and assemble thirty copies of each:

- Draft Bylaws (excluding the Draft Constitution) – Appendix B
- Alternate Bylaws Wording – Appendix C
- Subgroup Notes – Appendix D (It is necessary to identify the current constitution and bylaws wording and add the page number and article number of that wording to the notes sheet.)

Handouts in the appendices are available on a 3½ inch diskette. The files are already grouped in the format needed for the afternoon subgroup sessions—see Appendix G.

13. **Flipchart or overhead projector.** The work of the facilitator will be made easier if a large flipchart or overhead projector is available. Having both available is even better. Be sure that the flipchart has at least twenty unused pages. If an overhead projector is used you will want to have twenty

blank transparency sheets and several transparency pens.

14. **Technology.** Another key factor involves technology. Sometimes congregation leaders may not have the personal knowledge to secure the needed technology. In current times, all congregations have at least one person (often a teenager) capable of delivering the needed technological support.

Each subgroup will be developing text for a portion of the bylaws. As such, each subgroup needs a computer using the same word processing software. Most congregations can meet this technological need from within their membership. Once in a while it is necessary to borrow or rent the equipment.

The last session of the afternoon involves pulling together and displaying the work completed in the morning by the whole assembly, and by the five subgroups during the first half of the afternoon. Photocopying or reading text will not work when the event is completed in one day.

Thus, the main room needs a computer and LCD projector (sometimes called a PowerPoint® projector). This equipment allows the entire assembly to see the work they completed in the morning and the text developed by the subgroups in the afternoon.

15. **The day of the event.** The day of the event will be a wonder to behold. The congregation will experience great joy at completing what initially will seem impossible. More importantly, when the day is over, the congregation will have virtually all it needs to transform its constitution and bylaws into a flexible and missional document.

Sometimes people arrive at this point in the explanation and declare that the event is too complex and the objective cannot be achieved. Be assured that others have gone before you in accomplishing this event and achieving the goal. They come away from the process energized for ministry focused on spiritual growth of members and our Lord's Great Commission.

The most powerful component of the event does not have to be planned. No special arrangements or coordination is needed. It is automatic and free of cost.

The most powerful component of the event is that the Holy Spirit will guide the work. You will feel it in the room. You will see it in the group. You will hear it, even if some of the issues are controversial.

Chapter 6
Drafting a New Constitution

Chapter 6 lists the major decisions needed to create a new constitution that is flexible and missional. The chapter has two types of content:

1. Content in normal type presents the material on drafting a new constitution. The text can be used as a script for the facilitator leading a congregation meeting.
2. *Notes that explain background concepts are presented in italics. They are not intended for presentation to the assembly.*

Some denominations have a tradition that the local congregation does not have a constitution. Often their constitution exists in a book of rules and procedures prepared and maintained by the denomination. Churches with only bylaws will have to adjust the text presented in Chapter 6 by using the sections of this chapter (such as name and denominational affiliation) that match the corresponding content of their bylaws.

Most churches have a constitution and bylaws that are long and complex. Compare the constitution of your congregation with the constitution of St. Paul Church that is printed in Appendix A.

St. Paul Church has been using a flexible, missional constitution for fifteen years. During that time, the church has doubled in average weekly worship attendance and membership. They operate a school, early childhood center, ministries in the community, and missions in other countries. The ministry at St. Paul is typical of churches that have a strong relationship between effective Great Commission ministry and a flexible, missional constitution and bylaws.

The example constitution and bylaws of St. Paul Church represent one end of the spectrum of a flexible, missional structure. Most existing church constitutions and bylaws represent the opposite end of the spectrum.

Following the procedures suggested in this book will result in a document somewhere between these two extremes. Exactly where the new document falls is up to the congregation, not the authors of this book or the process facilitator.

Constitution decisions

In creating a new constitution, it is necessary to make between seven and twelve fundamental decisions. The example modeled in this chapter highlights ten of these decisions. It is not necessary during the event to deal with specific wording of the constitution or bylaws. These ten decisions shape the majority of the content of the constitution and require the judgment of the whole congregation.

In some churches, several of the questions posed in this chapter do not apply and should not be discussed. In other congregations one or two additional questions should be created to reflect required articles in constitutions. They need to be added to this list.

The actual number of fundamental decisions will be different in each congregation.

We start by considering four **major decisions**:

1. **Should the purpose remain the same?**
2. **Should the name remain the same?**
3. **Should the theological commitment remain the same?**
4. **Should the denominational affiliation remain the same?**

Examine the text at the beginning of the current constitution. Without wordsmithing the text, what do you feel is the answer to each of these four questions?

Discuss your judgment of each of these questions with one other person. In about two minutes we will take a "straw poll" to see what people think.

The order of presenting these first four decisions may need to be changed. It should match the order in which they appear in the current constitution or bylaws.

Ask everyone to examine the appropriate section from the current constitution and discuss these four questions with one other person.

Conducting these discussions in teams of two, not a whole table together, is <u>very important</u>. Teams of two permit everyone to state their opinion in a minute or two. Normally the teams of two consist of the same person from the earlier discussion about sprinter or marathon runner.

Many will be tempted to conduct whole table discussions. When whole tables of six or eight people attempt to discuss each question, it takes more time than is appropriate and not everyone gets to express themselves either because of lack of time or being intimidated. The facilitator may need to roam around the room encouraging groups to limit their discussion to teams of two people.

What are your answers? By a show of hands, how many feel that the purpose should generally remain the same? We are not adjusting the specific wording at this time. We only want to get an idea about the overall direction.

How many feel it should be dramatically changed?

In most churches the overwhelming majority will be comfortable with the current general statement of the church's purpose. Most are written so broadly that objection is not necessary.

If a significant number of people seek a change, then ask them to express their thoughts in a general way. Do not permit "tweaking" of words and phrases. Pay attention to what is said, but do not let it bog down the flow.

A "significant number" should be at least twenty percent of those attending. Do not let one or two strong-willed people stop the process. If

they persist, simply point out the overwhelming, lopsided vote and move on.

If there is energy to make change, there will also be energy to remain unchanged. Record the various points of view on a flipchart or overhead projector. Collect a listing but do not permit debate. Opportunity for debate will come later.

Again, most people in most congregations will be sufficiently satisfied with the thrust of the current wording.

By a show of hands, how many feel that the congregation's name should remain the same? How many feel it should be changed?

How many feel that the theological commitment should remain the same? How many feel it should be changed?

How many feel the denominational affiliation should remain the same?

In most congregations, there is no objection to these first four questions. If there are objections, simply collect the various thoughts and keep moving. Decisions are not needed now because the majority of the content of the rest of the constitution and bylaws cover internal procedures that are largely independent of these first four questions.

Most congregation members answer "yes" to all of the first four questions. That realization is important. The first four questions cover what the congregation is and what it stands for.

It is important to notice that nothing is being changed about these fundamental perceptions. What the congregation stands for will continue. The remainder of the constitution and bylaws are only about how the congregation will operate.

This insight will be important to a number of participants who will be very nervous about this process. It is important for them to hear that the core of what the church is will not be changed.

5. **Is a Lay Leadership Group to be responsible for implementing the overall ministry of the congregation as determined by the Voters?**

The next question comes directly from the earlier presentations on structure. Should we have a Lay Leadership Group that is responsible for implementing the overall ministry of the congregation? Remember that this group is responsible for implementing, not for creating. The congregation determines the overall ministry plan, the specific outcomes, and the budgets.

At this point we will not deal with the name of this group, who is in the group, or how they get to those positions. That will all be handled later. The only question is whether we want to have such a group as described earlier.

Ask the assembly to discuss this with their team partner. Discourage whole-table discussions.

Some congregations may claim they already have this exact type of Lay Leadership Group. An important factor in the suggested approach is that being on the Lay Leadership Group comes from election at large, not from leading a board or committee.

For other churches, this approach is different from their current arrangement, and a few people may need to hear some of the characteristics of this new concept. Simply repeat the main points from the Lay Leadership Group section of Chapter 4.

The teams of two might need up to three minutes for discussion.

By a show of hands, how many feel the church should have a Lay Leadership Group that is responsible for implementing the decisions of the Voters?

How many prefer some other arrangement?

6. Should the Lay Leadership Group have authority to create and recreate structure to achieve the Voter-defined ministry?

The next question comes from the reality that responsibility for outcomes must be accompanied by authority to take action. The question is whether or not the Lay Leadership Group should have the authority to create and recreate structures needed to achieve the Voter-defined ministry.

This does not mean that all existing boards, committees, and methods are automatically eliminated. It simply means that the Lay Leadership Group is authorized to adjust the structure as times, needs, and resources change without

calling a Voters' meeting to amend the constitution or bylaws.

Take about two minutes to discuss this question with your team partner.

By a show of hands, how many feel that the Lay Leadership Group should have authority to create and recreate structure needed to achieve the Voter-defined ministry?

In most congregations, this will be overwhelmingly accepted. As before, if a significant number of participants object (at least twenty percent), record their opinions and move on. In the unlikely event that the assembly is evenly divided, then it is necessary to stop the process and work on this question. Much of the remainder of the process depends upon an affirmative reply to this question.

Virtually all congregations will overwhelmingly approve this concept. In so doing, half to three-quarters of the current bylaws are eliminated—quickly and easily.

7. Should the day school board be responsible to the Voters or to the Lay Leadership Group?

Question 7 is a model for congregations that have a major program or activity so large that it is often separately incorporated. It might be a day school, child care center, halfway house, nursing home, major foundation, or other substantial enterprise that is part of the overall ministry, but not necessarily under the congregation's leadership structure.

Most churches will skip Question 7. It should be skipped in both of the following situations:

1. *If governmental statutes or articles of incorporation already require that the major program or activity be independent of the Lay Leadership Group.*

2. *If the major program/activity's current oversight group already reports to the Lay Leadership Group.*

The next critical question is whether the day school board should be accountable directly to the Voters or to the Lay Leadership Group. The ideas described in the earlier sections all support the notion that the day school board should be accountable to the Lay Leadership Group. However, some churches prefer a parallel structure even though it is not recommended.

Take about two minutes to discuss this choice with your team partner.

By a show of hands, how many feel that the day school board should be responsible to the Lay Leadership Group?

How many feel it should be responsible to the Voters and not to the Lay Leadership Group?

Most congregations place the day school board under the Lay Leadership Group. In the rare instance where they pick the Voters and not the Lay Leadership Group, then an additional subgroup is needed for the afternoon to prepare a bylaw section covering the day school board.

8. Should the congregation require a Board of Elders or shall that decision be left to the Lay Leadership Group?

If the congregation does not already have a Board of Elders or similar clergy oversight group, the question should be skipped.

In some denominations, churches traditionally have groups sometimes called Elders. Normally, this group is said to have responsibility for the spiritual health of the congregation. Often this group is charged with visiting attending members, calling on delinquent members, managing the membership lists, supervising worship services, assisting the pastor in some ecclesiastical duties, sometimes having authority over the pastor in spiritual matters, and a host of other responsibilities.

Mostly Boards of Elders attend the monthly meetings and handle their mechanical duties. Our research shows that most members feel that Elders are generally ineffective at visiting members and not at all involved in calling on delinquent members. Most members of Boards of Elders agree with that assessment. It is not unusual for people to be elected to a Board of Elders for reasons that have little to do with the ability to call on people with love and compassion.

Another aspect of Boards of Elders is a critical element of the new approach to leadership described earlier. The concept is that no individual should be accountable to more than one group. Serious issues often emerge when the Senior Pastor is responsible to the Lay Leadership Group for some things and to a Board of Elders for others.

It is also the case that many churches are having difficulty finding people willing to serve on the Board of Elders.

Previously, the congregation decided that the Lay Leadership Group is authorized to create the structure needed to carry out the ministry selected by the Voters. This gives the Lay Leadership Group authority to break up the traditional list of duties normally assigned to the Board of Elders into smaller teams of people more skilled in the specific needs. For example, a visiting team calls on shut-ins. The most experienced members of the visiting team call on delinquent members. A different team can assist with worship.

Thus, it is clear that there are a lot of reasons why the existence of a Board of Elders is best decided by the Lay Leadership Group. However, this is a critical issue and should be thought about and decided by the congregation. Please discuss it with your team partner for two minutes.

By a show of hands, how many feel the decision about a Board of Elders should be left to the Lay Leadership Group?

How many feel that the congregation should require a Board of Elders?

9. Should the Voters have authority to terminate employment of a called worker?

Even if already permitted by the existing structure, there is value is reaffirming this point.

Sometimes there are questions about exactly how this happens. Respond that the details will be worked out in the afternoon session.

In some traditions this is not allowed. A called worker either has that call for life or until released at their request. In other traditions only a person of authority outside the congregation can terminate a divine call.

Begin by stating whatever the case is in the tradition of the church.

This is a major point that should be discussed and voted on by the group. Please take two minutes to discuss this question with your team partner.

By a show of hands, how many feel that the Voters should have the authority to terminate employment of a called worker?

How many are opposed?

10. If there is a split in the church, should the property remain with the majority?

As with question number nine, this issue may already be stipulated in the current constitution as just suggested. However, it is a major issue and should be reviewed during this time of revising the constitution and bylaws.

This last point recognizes a reality of the court system that is different from the provisions in a large number of church constitutions or recommendations by denominations. Many constitutions stipulate that if a split occurs, the property remains with the group holding to the articles of faith listed in the constitution or to some sort of statement about "purity of doctrine." No governmental courts will mediate any disagreement related to faith, doctrine, or belief. Churches relying on adherence to a particular faith position to settle a property dispute during a split are headed for a disaster worse than the congregational split itself.

The suggested wording is clear and easy to interpret. It is enforceable by a governmental court.

Some of us are uncomfortable discussing this issue now. Be assured it is better to make a decision at a time when the congregation is not embroiled in bitter dispute. Take two minutes to discuss this matter with your team partner.

How many feel that in the event that the congregation splits, the property should remain with the majority?

How many feel differently?

We have now made all the decisions necessary to create a draft of the church's constitution. Later this afternoon an initial draft will be displayed for consideration.

Chapter 7
Drafting New Bylaws

Chapter 7 describes how to draft the bylaws. Some of the specific details below will be different in the various denominations. Other details will need modest modification to fit the church and the major decisions made by the assembly. The format can easily be adapted to fit most situations.

Appendices B, C, and D contain materials useful to the subgroups. These materials will greatly reduce the amount of time the subgroup needs without limiting the nature of their consideration. They are also available on a 3½ inch diskette in Microsoft® Word 97 (see Appendix G.)

Bylaws Decisions

Bylaws describe the way the congregation is organized and operates. They list who can participate in various ways, and provide fundamental statements about decision-making.

The prior session covered key questions related to the constitution and also made several **decisions affecting the bylaws**. The key decisions that affect the bylaws are:

1. We will have a Lay Leadership Group.
2. The Lay Leadership Group will define the structure.
3. We will not require a Board of Elders.
4. The Voters will have authority to terminate employment of a called worker.

Having made these decisions, the bylaws need to cover five areas. In a few minutes the assembly will be divided into five subgroups. Each subgroup will consider bylaws content in one of the areas. Each person is asked to select one of the five areas. As they are described, be thinking about which subgroup you would like to join.

The first subgroup will develop thoughts and wording on **membership**. They will deal with the different types of member, methods of becoming a member, and issues on terminating membership.

The second subgroup will deal with **voting**. This includes such things as who is eligible to vote, when and how often regular meetings will be held, procedures for special meetings, and the minimum number of Voters needed to make decisions.

The third subgroup will handle matters related to **called workers**. This does not include all employees. It only involves those issued a call by the congregation as a whole. The discussion will cover eligibility, methods for issuing the call, and procedures for terminating employment of a called worker.

The fourth subgroup will discuss the titles, duties, election, and removal from office of the congregation's **officers**.

The final subgroup will talk about the name for this group, how many are in the group, their primary responsibilities, and the role of the Senior Pastor in the **Lay Leadership Group**.

Invite the assembly to scan the list and make a preliminary selection. Give them about one minute. Then tell them we want to get an estimate of the number of people who want to deal with each topic. Ask how many want to participate in each.

Another person could then determine subgroup room assignments while the facilitator finishes the orientation. The room assignments can be written on a flipchart or on an overhead projector transparency to be displayed after the remaining points are provided.

Each person in the subgroup will receive a set of **background materials on the bylaws** your group will be discussing. Following the suggestions in the materials will help the subgroup give their topic careful consideration, without taking more time than is needed.

The first sheet in the subgroup materials is a **list of the major questions the subgroup needs to consider**. Sticking to these questions will help keep the subgroup from becoming diverted by small matters that probably do not require the entire subgroup's attention.

It is usually more efficient for a large group to be working from **draft text to get started** than from a blank piece of paper. Therefore, the second helpful aid in the subgroup materials is a draft of possible wording. The draft is not required text. It simply helps the group have a starting place.

You already have the third set of helpful materials. It is **the current constitution and bylaws**. The first page of the subgroup materials gives the location of the subgroup's content in the current document.

As was indicated earlier, the flexible, missional approach to constitutions and bylaws has already been accomplished at other churches. The final portion of the subgroup materials contains examples of how **other congregations have worded** the material being considered by the subgroup.

Subgroup tasks

After you get into your subgroup room please complete the following four activities. Spend only a small amount of time on the first three and almost all of your time on the fourth:

1. Read the list of major questions
2. Read the draft wording
3. Read the current document
4. Answer the major questions

Sometimes groups tend to jump around, carrying on several conversations at once. It will be helpful to deal with each one of the questions before going on to the next.

During the final two minutes **select someone to report the major concepts** to the whole group when we return back to this room. The report will not be polished and it simply explains the major decisions made or points of view if a decision was not reached.

These final thoughts before breaking into the subgroups will help you make progress and avoid getting bogged down.

Discuss questions in teams of two. Sometimes there is a tendency for the whole group to want to talk together about each question. Remember how many major decisions we made this morning by starting with discussion in teams of two? The same is true for this afternoon. It will be more helpful to discuss each question by starting with teams of two people sharing their views for one or two minutes.

After the discussion in teams of two, it will be easier to concisely **share the major thoughts** with the whole subgroup. Often the subgroup will quickly reach consensus and can move on to the next question.

After surfacing the major points of view, take a **straw poll**, just a quick show of hands, to see how many people support each of the points of view. Often the vote is strongly for one of the options, in which case the group is ready to move on.

The goals in the subgroups are to **make preliminary decisions or capture major options**. If the vote is evenly divided, then see if a little more discussion will achieve consensus. If it seems that consensus will take a long time or not be possible, then simply record the major points of difference for reporting to the whole group later and move on to the next question.

We are now ready to move into the **subgroup meeting rooms**.

Announce the subgroup meeting room locations. These can be displayed on a flipchart or on an overhead projector.

After the first room assignment is announced, again ask for a show of hands of those going to the first subgroup.

Ask for someone in the subgroup familiar with Microsoft® Word to come forward to receive the subgroup materials and diskette on which they are to record the subgroup's decisions. Repeat for all five subgroups.

IT IS NOT NECESSARY TO APPOINT A CHAIR OF THE SUBGROUP DISCUSSIONS.

Each subgroup will handle this need in the manner most comfortable for them.

Announce that the subgroups can start the afternoon break when they have finished their deliberations.

Announce the time at which the whole group will reassemble after their deliberations and break. In most cases, sixty minutes is enough time to reach consensus or identify the major points to be brought back to the whole group.

After these announcements, dismiss the assembly to their subgroup sessions.

Give the subgroups about five minutes to get settled. The facilitator should make one short visit to each subgroup location. Sometimes it is helpful to encourage them to follow the suggested procedures printed at the top of the first page of their subgroup materials.

The point is to give them a procedure that helps them keep moving without feeling like they are being stampeded. Three things are key to helping them keep from becoming bogged down:

1. *Encourage them to start the consideration of each question with a team-of-two discussion.*

2. *Use frequent straw polls to differentiate between a true impasse and one or two strong-willed people holding the majority hostage to their clearly minority point of view.*

3. *If a true impasse occurs, simply record both points of view to be brought before the whole assembly.*

After making an initial round of the subgroup meetings, there will be time to adjust the wording of the draft constitution to match the morning discussion.

About thirty minutes after the session starts, make another round of visits to be sure the subgroups have not become bogged down. They need to cover all their questions in the time available, even if they are not able to reach closure on each.

Chapter 8
Bringing Constitution and Bylaws Together

Chapter 8 describes the method used to help the entire assembly bring together a preliminary draft of the constitution and bylaws. An experienced facilitator will not need a suggested script.

After welcoming the group back into the room, immediately launch into the draft constitution. It is not necessary for people to have their own copy. Displaying the text on the screen is sufficient.

Someone will need to load the subgroup diskette into the computer and display the text on the screen. This can be the facilitator. It can be someone else—possibly a teenager. It must be someone at least modestly skilled with Microsoft® Word.

Use Microsoft® Word, not PowerPoint®, to directly display the text. For ease of viewing, we recommend the following:

1. *Arial font style at size 12.*
2. *Remove all toolbars, except Standard.*
3. *Adjust the Zoom to a percentage that leaves each line width matching the width of the display.*
4. *If you use the scroll key to move text up or down, scroll slowly so people do not get lost or become dizzy.*

Display Article I at the top of the screen and comment that no changes have been made or that the decided changes have been made.

Do the same for each article in which no changes have been made. This is usually the purpose, name, denominational affiliation, and statements on doctrine. Emphasize again that the core of what the congregation is will remain unchanged.

Display constitution articles where major changes were made. Point them out, pause to see if there are comments, and move on.

Watch the time and keep moving. The subgroup reports are critical and will take at least a full hour.

Skip any constitution articles that contain decisions covered by bylaws subgroups. For example, some constitutions have brief statements defining membership that are further defined in the bylaws.

Once in a while an issue will surface on which there seems to be divided opinion. The "straw poll" technique is a powerful way of assessing the true feelings of the assembly without calling for a formal decision. A straw poll is an informal show of hands. Most people, including the strong-willed people dominating the discussion, will be comfortable with this approach.

The best way to describe usage and impact of this approach is with an example. A group was discussing the name of their church. Several speakers suggested "St. Luke Church," an equal number pushed for "St. Luke Church and School," and another group wanted "St. Luke Ministries."

The facilitator listed on an overhead the advantages and disadvantages cited by the speakers as they made strong cases for their preferences. The room seemed evenly divided and headed for an impasse.

The facilitator told the assembly that a straw poll would be taken. The group was given one minute to discuss the choices with their team partner. A show of hands vote was taken.

More than eighty people voted for "St. Luke Church," about a dozen (led by the school principal) voted for "St. Luke Church and School," and only the three people who spoke for "St. Luke Ministries" voted for that option.

The straw poll kept the group going. It also achieved two important outcomes. First, it showed that the assembly was firmly on one side of the issue. Second, it ended the discussion by showing the dissenters that they were a small minority.

This second outcome is critical. In many congregations there is a small cluster of people who literally hold the majority hostage to their own point of view. Because they only discuss their perspective with a few friends, they have the impression that their viewpoint reflects a large portion of the church. The straw poll approach is an effective way of releasing the majority from the tyranny of a few strong-willed people.

Article XI of the draft constitution (Appendix B) contains language about changing the constitution. If the congregation's current constitution contains language that is functional in current times, it should be inserted into the draft being displayed. If the provided draft is different from the current constitution, be sure to point out the differences.

Congratulate the assembly on creating a preliminary draft of a new constitution. Indicate that the wording will be checked and cleaned.

The next step in the process is to receive reports from the subgroups. Ask the spokesperson to come forward with their diskette. Load the diskette and display it on the screen. Ask the spokesperson to briefly summarize each section. Use the computer cursor (mouse) to point to text being referenced by the speaker.

Sometimes the subgroup will indicate they were not able to reach consensus. Ask the spokesperson to summarize the main points of view. It will be helpful to list those points on the flipchart or overhead projector.

Ask for comments from the floor, recording on the flipchart or overhead any additional thoughts. Try to limit the discussion from the floor to new thoughts or points of view not already expressed.

After all points have been expressed, announce that a straw poll will be taken. The facilitator briefly summarizes the major thoughts on each point of view. Give the assembly no more than a minute to contemplate their choice and then conduct the straw poll.

Commonly the assembly will vote strongly (seventy-five percent or more) for one of the points of view. When that happens, the issue has been decided. Do not permit further discussion. Move on to the next point.

If the vote is more evenly divided (e.g., sixty percent on one point of view), announce that further discussion will be needed at a later time and move on.

Once in a while, someone will object that those voting on these issues at the event are not eligible to vote under the current constitution's rules for changing the constitution. Calmly point out that this event is simply drafting new wording, not installing the actual changes. That will happen at a later time and using the process required in the current constitution and bylaws.

Work your way through the five groups. Be aware of the clock and keep moving.

When all subgroups have reported, announce that the task of drafting a new constitution and bylaws has been mostly completed. Indicate that specific "wordsmithing" will occur and that announcements will be made about the time of the formal revision voting procedure.

Thank the steering committee.

Thank the food team, child care team, and any others who played key roles.

Thank everyone for attending, congratulation everyone for a job well done. Call on the person conducting the closing devotion.

Chapter 9
Transition From Current to New

Chapter 9 describes one way to complete the formal transition from the current constitution and bylaws to the new document. Perhaps the most important aspect of the conversion is to be sure that the procedures in the current constitution are followed. These usually include rules about notification of the meeting at which the vote will be taken and the percentage needed to approve the new document.

Following the procedures in the current constitution is necessary, even though it may be difficult, frustrating, or time-consuming. If procedures are not observed, then it only takes one disgruntled person to stop or delay the process.

After completing the event, the congregation will have a draft of a new constitution. It will need cleaning by a knowledgeable person who enjoys the confidence of the majority in the congregation. Often the event facilitator has that trust and can do the "wordsmithing." Sometimes another trusted person will finish the document.

Sometimes the event produces an issue on which there is a small (twenty percent or less) minority point of view. Generally, such issues should not consume any special effort to reach consensus. Although it is helpful for everyone to be supportive, it is not helpful for anyone to feel empowered to prevent the congregation from adopting a course of action to which that individual and a small group of friends object. Simply insert the wording preferred by the clear majority and proceed with the final version of the document.

Once in a great while a particularly sticky issue will surface with more than twenty percent holding a minority point of view. It is important to attempt to settle the issue before the final ratification vote, but not during the one-day event. One method of dealing with the issue is to create an action team made up of everyone interested in the topic. Give that group not more than one month to come up with wording acceptable to as many as possible. Usually this action team will accomplish the task in the suggested timeframe.

If the action team is not able to reach agreement, the congregation leaders have to make a difficult choice. One option is to delay the final vote until the matter can be resolved. Usually that means involving an outside mediator. The other option is to present the issues to the congregation at a separate gathering prior to the final ratification vote.

We recommend that the congregation's leaders take care in scheduling the timing of the final ratification vote. It should occur when the most eligible voters can attend. The general rule is to avoid the temptation to move "as quickly as possible." If there are contentious issues and the ratification vote occurs at an inconvenient time, it is entirely possible for a highly motivated minority to defeat the ratification. In addition, it is just good leadership to be sure that as many people who can vote will have the opportunity to do so.

In most situations, the ratification vote can occur between six weeks and three months after the event. Usually it is better to hold the ratification vote at a properly called special meeting at which nothing else will be discussed. Using the procedures defined in this book normally results in overwhelming approval, without need for discussion.

If a few strong-willed people seek to block the will of the majority, remember the power of the "straw vote" procedure. Use it on the sole point being objected to, announce that the matter is settled, and move on.

Sometimes the final ratification meeting results in an approval, followed by a motion to make the decision unanimous. We recommend avoiding this practice. The enthusiasm that creates the suggestion is understandable; however, the action is not necessary and can easily embarrasses those who do not agree. We recommend a celebration worship experience begin immediately after the approval vote is taken and before anyone ask that the decision be made unanimous.

Ratification of the new document usually implies implementation of a new structure. If the structural characteristics in the model constitution are adopted, there will be major changes. In many congregations the Lay Leadership Group will be a different collection of people than those currently serving.

A helpful way of dealing with the transition is to ratify the new constitution and bylaws, and at the same time adopt an implementation resolution. The implementation resolution would generally be structured as in this example:

2/1 – Ratify the new constitution and bylaws

2/8 – The current Nominating Committee creates a slate of candidates for officers and Lay Leadership Group

3/1 – The Voters defined by the new constitution and bylaws elect the officers and Lay Leadership Group

5/1 – The Lay Leadership Group meets in retreat for leadership training and creation of the new structure

6/1 – The new constitution and bylaws officially replace the current document.

The transition will be smoother if scheduled during a time that will be the least disruptive to ministries. Changing structure at the beginning of the church activity year will likely create confusion, particularly in decision-making.

Of course, the transition can be handled in a variety of ways. The point is that the ratification vote is the simplest part of the process. The two challenges are how to create the new structure and what the new structure will be.

The natural tendency is to spend many hours in discussion in order to discover the fine-tuned, fully-coordinated, well-oiled structure that will be perfect and permanent. We invite you to give up this tendency. A more helpful way forward is to put in place a minimum of structure, with the focus on developing people as they discover their God-given talents and gifts. In other words, the structure will be defined by the ministry—not the other way around.

Sometimes a person experienced in newer approaches to leading volunteer organizations can provide helpful training.

An important part of the current thinking on leading volunteer organizations is creation of a Policy Manual. Chapter 10 provides a draft for the Lay Leadership Group and all boards, committees, task forces, action teams, and any other entity of the church. This manual displays the key concepts of Carver and others.

The good news about creating the new structure is embedded within the basic concept. Simply put, nothing is written in concrete and everything is easy to adjust.

Do not overlook what currently is working. It is totally appropriate to go to a group that is currently functioning effectively and ask them to be the "new" group.

The challenge is to deal with those aspects of the congregation's ministry that are not functioning effectively. In these situations, the Lay Leadership Group might be able to create an effective replacement idea right away. In other situations, the current ministry group might be asked to continue and to participate in discussions about a successor arrangement.

Tact is required in this type of situation. Avoid letting over-enthusiasm crush motivated and well-intentioned people who are conducting an activity whose time may have passed. Sometimes haste can create a bad taste about how the transitions were handled.

Completing the transition to a new structure and function can be the most challenging part of the whole process. This is particularly true if the new structure is dramatically different from the current situation.

The last two chapters of this book provide helpful aids in this process.

Chapter 10
Operating Procedures

The leadership of the congregation (Senior Pastor and Congregation Chair) will have a number of questions about the specifics of getting started. Most concerns will be for the activities of the Lay Leadership Group. Some are for the relationships between the various boards, committees, action teams, and paid staff. There are a number of general guidelines and some specific suggestions:

General Guidelines

1. Keep the Lay Leadership Group focused on the overall objectives of the congregation. Avoid the natural tendency to slip into the old way of doing things, tying up the meeting with operational details.
2. Let the various existing boards and committees play a major role in sorting out the new structure. They will have a good sense of what to do and just need encouragement to be creative.
3. Avoid loading the Senior Pastor with the need to be involved in operational details. (In some cases, the Senior Pastor may need encouragement to do the opposite of what was taught in seminary.)

This third general guideline deserves elaboration before getting into the specific suggestions. A critical principle for a congregation to experience Great Commission success is that the congregation's most potent ministry person needs to be in the mission field. There are several ways of expressing this idea.

Kennon Callahan offers three helpful suggestions. "Spend one hour in the mission field for every minute of preaching time." This is not a plea for short sermons. It is an encouragement to get out of the office and be in the mission field. At first, some pastors will have difficulty with this notion. A few parishioners will complain that the "pastor is not in the office." The unspoken but often felt conclusion of that thought is "…to take care of me at my convenience." Being in the mission field helps the pastor know how to be the missional leader. Interestingly, sermon preparation time drops precipitously when the pastor spends more time in the mission field than in the office.

"If the pastor knows everything that is going on, then not enough is going on." During the days of the church culture, the rhythm of the congregation was pretty much the same from one year to the next. The pastor spent large amounts of time monitoring the repeated activities. Changes were minor and infrequent. On a mission field the key is being responsive to needs in the mission field and missional yearnings that our Lord places on the hearts of members. Both factors require flexibility. In a congregation that is active in the mission field, the pastor simply cannot be involved in everything.

"If the pastor needs to know everything, the ministry will be limited to that over which the pastor can personally say grace." This reality flies in the face of virtually everything that most pastors are taught. And yet, this simple quotation makes perfect sense. Some pastors will have a hard time "just letting go." The word of hope is that on the other side of control is the wonderful blessing of the Holy Spirit (not the pastor) controlling the direction of the ministry.

Several specific suggestions will help the congregation make a good start. They will also relieve the leaders of the natural tendency to be worried about the unknown.

First LLG Meeting – Topic 1 (30 minutes)

The first meeting of the Lay Leadership Group will set the tone for a new way of doing things. There are three (sometimes four) topics for that meeting and many things that are not on the agenda.

Begin the meeting with a prayer and solid Bible study on the purpose of the church. This is not the usual "God bless this meeting and let's get started." This first thirty minutes in Bible study is very important. Prayer can include intercessions and thanksgiving. This book intentionally does not suggest the Biblical basis because it is important for the meeting leaders to search and locate the scriptural text for themselves. It is very important that the professional staff avoid creating and conducting this opening time of considering God's Word. The pastor can suggest three or four scriptural references, but should express verbal support for the ability of the chair and/or vice chair to create and conduct this opening.

First LLG Meeting – Topic 2 (10 minutes)

The second agenda item deals with Lay Leadership Group officers and terms of office, and should only take about ten minutes. Most churches name the congregation Chairperson as the chair of the Lay Leadership Group, but some will leave that to the Group itself. A standard nomination and secret ballot can be used to select the group leadership roles.

Most new constitutions will indicate the desire for staggered terms of office for at-large Lay Leadership Group members. If that was not handled during the election process, then the Biblical method of "drawing lots" should be used. For example, if the congregation has created five Group members elected to three-year terms, then a drawing is held for one term that expires in one year and two that expire in two years. The remaining terms expire in three years.

First LLG Meeting – Topic 3 (30 minutes)

The third topic is to quickly review each of the current boards and committees. If this activity takes more than thirty minutes, the Lay Leadership Group is being too analytical.

Separate the boards and committees into two groups. Group A consists of those groups that are doing a reasonably good job at the activity they are intended to be doing (which may not be what they are actually doing). For example, if the building and grounds are reasonably well maintained (in the eyes of a first-time worshipper, not us) then the Board of Properties is placed into Group A.

Those that are not doing reasonably well at the activity they are intended to be doing would be placed in Group B. Do not spend a lot of time debating the details. Try to step back and take an overall assessment. Above all, avoid the temptation to discuss what they should do to fix their performance. That important discussion is not an appropriate discussion for the Lay Leadership Group at this time.

The important thing in distinguishing between Groups A and B is the concept of doing the activity they are intended to do. They may be doing well, but it may not be that which they are intended to do. The best way to explain this difference is with two examples:

1. The Evangelism Committee may be putting on a wonderful annual congregation-wide potluck meal. However, if the number of first-time worshippers is small in relationship to the community's size, then the Evangelism Committee is placed in Group B.
2. The Elders may be doing an excellent job of being sure that the lights are on for worship, the usher teams are fully staffed, and there are no disruptions during worship. But, if the shut-ins and infrequent attenders are not being visited, then the Elders are not doing what they are primarily intended to be doing. They are placed in Group B.

This sorting process should not be allowed to take more than thirty minutes. Avoid the tendency to want to diagnose and extensively discuss. Simply sort the boards and committees into either of two groups.

Two different types of communications are to be sent to these two groups. Group A will receive a letter (or email) from the secretary inviting those boards and committees to think about how they can best structure their work. Each Group A board or committee is asked to recommend:

1. How best to be organized (as is, form multiple subgroups, divide into multiple action teams).
2. How best to function (when to meet, how to select a chair).
3. How to reconstitute themselves. These should mostly be self-appointed and almost never elected by the congregation as a whole.
4. Which other boards, committees, task forces, action teams, and staff they should routinely relate to and how best to do that.

Each unit in Group A is invited to take not more than three months to report their decisions in written form to the Lay Leadership Group. The format of this report should be concise and should be consistent for all boards and committees. The secretary or chair may wish to create a format. The chair may wish to appoint someone to create a format. The entire Lay Leadership Group should not discuss the report format. One or two people can make that decision.

Under no circumstances should any pastor be involved in any way in creating this format or managing the details of this process. Some pastors will be tempted to say, "It is easier for me to do it than to explain it." Others will say, "this needs to be done right, so I better do it." A few will feel strongly drawn to the "need" to be involved in this step so that they "know what is going on." All of these indicate problems with perfectionism or control. A few Senior Pastors might need the help of the elected volunteer leadership to feel comfortable "letting this go."

Each unit that is placed into Group B will need one or two members of the Lay Leadership Group to contact the leader of a Group B board or committee. This contact is to communicate a few suggestions and is not to continue to attend their meetings to guide their activity.

The communication to Group B boards and committees would ask them to do four things:

1. Create a short list of the primary ministry goals they are to be accomplishing. This is not the list of what they are doing. It is a list of what they are to be accomplishing. Some will have a hard time seeing this distinction.
2. For each entry create a short self-evaluation of how they are doing in accomplishing their primary function. Encourage the board or committee members to be fair and honest with themselves.
3. Ask the board or committee to think about how they might like to reorganize themselves to accomplish the primary ministry intended. Be sure that they are aware that disbanding their function is an option.
4. Ask the board or committee to select one or two people to summarize the third point and communicate their insights to the Lay Leadership Group. This communication should be in writing so that Lay Leadership Group can read the report and not be forced to hear a time-consuming oral presentation.

First LLG Meeting – Topic 4 (60 minutes)

The fourth major activity is critical and will take about an hour. The primary reason for creating the Lay Leadership Group is to focus on how the congregation is doing in ministry.

An important distinction to bear in mind is that this conversation is not intended to create the list of ministry outcomes for the congregation. Rather, it is to understand the question well enough that the various choices can be brought to the whole congregation for their discussion and decision.

A helpful place to start is an open discussion of what might be used to assess ministry impact. These can be listed and briefly discussed. Some examples are:

1. **Average weekly worship attendance.** Do not use total membership. Average worship attendance is a measure of participation and is more helpful than measures of affiliation.
2. **Number of persons served in mission.** This concept refers to nonmembers whose lives

are touched in meaningful ways in the name of the congregation. Examples of people included in this count are nonmember children and their families in the preschool, homeless persons who come to the church for a meal, and those who attend the recovery groups led by church members. Examples of good things congregations do that are not included are donations to a community center food pantry and renting building space to another organization to conduct a helping activity.

3. **Number of members directly involved in delivering first person ministry on behalf of and in the name of the congregation.** This is not the number of people who attend meetings, because meetings are not ministry. Meetings can sometimes be helpful to prepare for delivering ministry.

4. **Number of adults confirmed or baptized in a year.** These individuals are those who are new to the faith or who have returned after a long absence. It does not include people who transfer into the congregation from another congregation.

5. **Average weekly number of people participating in Bible study.** This count is not limited to classes that meet in the church buildings.

6. **Percentage of meeting time spent in the Lay Leadership Group meetings to discuss the overall ministry of the congregation.** Time is often a more precious commodity than money. The way people spend their time directly reflects their priorities. Similarly, the way an organization's leadership spends its time directly reflects upon the priorities of the organization.

   A church's leadership that spends the majority of its time on "inside the church" matters reflects an internally focused congregation. When the leaders spend the majority of their time dealing with "reaching out to broken and hurting people with a healing Jesus," the congregation lives out the Great Commission.

7. **Percentage of the total congregation budget spent directly on the Great Commission in our community, nation, and the world.** Just as how we spend time reflects on total mission, so to does the way the church spends its money. The amount that a church spends on itself or on reaching others directly reflects the true mission of the church.

The direction of the outreach percentage is as important as the amount itself. Many congregations pride themselves on giving a "percent of total receipts" to missions. At the same time, they ignore that over a decade or so the percentage has been allowed to decrease. At the very least, the percentage of total income spent on outreach should be the same from year to year. More helpful is for the percentage to steadily increase to a desired, substantial amount. Congregations are well advised to practice what they are teaching to the members about stewardship.

A caution is important about the congregation's calculation of the amount it spends on outreach. The amount should be substantially more than the dollars sent in the checks to worthy causes. The total spent on outreach should include the allocated cost of time and other expenses of paid staff and facilities.

The suggestion of fully allocated spending in ministry areas is far too large for this chapter. Kennon Callahan's book, *Effective Church Finances*, contains an excellent discussion in the first chapter, "A Mission Budget." The key difference from current practice is that the mission budget is displayed in ministry areas such as local outreach, youth programs, children's ministries, and so forth. The staff and overhead costs of those activities are included within the ministry budget, and not lumped into a line item called "personnel."

The brainstorming portion of this one-hour segment will be an interesting discussion that should not be allowed to take more than thirty minutes. The purpose of the brainstorming is not to prepare to tell the congregation what the ministry outcomes should be. The purpose is to understand the topic well enough to discern how to create a congregation-wide gathering where they can make those decisions.

The second half of the one-hour ministry outcomes discussion at this first Lay Leadership Group meeting is to discuss when and how to hold the congregation-wide meeting. One or two Lay Leadership Group members will be needed to lead the Ministry Outcomes Meeting Action Team. Additional action team members can be added from the congregation's general membership. This group is empowered to create the event. Hopefully the All-Congregation Ministry Outcomes meeting can occur within about three months. The congregation decisions will be needed by the Lay Leadership Group as it reviews the plans and procedures being decided by the various boards, committees, and action teams.

First LLG Meeting – Topic 5 (15 minutes)

The final topic for the first Lay Leadership Group meeting is a fifteen-minute discussion about the content of the Consent Agenda. The Consent Agenda is a list of the routine information that will be distributed to Lay Leadership Group members about seven days prior to regular meetings. The items on the agenda are not discussed during the meeting unless a major problem appears to be developing.

Examples of matters on the Consent Agenda are:
1. Official acts
2. Financial reports
3. Participation reports
4. Periodic annual reports from boards, committees, action teams, etc.

Summary

During the first several Lay Leadership Group meetings, there will be a tendency to feel the need to hear and discuss routine matters. This is a habit from the days of paying attention to details and missing the big picture. The members of the Lay Leadership Group should be generally aware of the information via the Consent Agenda. The Lay Leadership Group is responsible for seeing that actions are taken if any of these normal functions start to become problems. Again, remember that "seeing that actions are

taken" does not mean formal intervention by the group.

The most important matter for the Lay Leadership Group is to spend at least half of every meeting on the general topic of whether the congregation is achieving its objectives in ministry. This activity includes:

- Helping the congregation select ministry direction and outcomes;
- Creating the organization needed to achieve the direction and outcomes;
- Helping the boards, committees, and action teams include the overall ministry direction and outcomes; and
- Assuring that the Lay Leadership Group stays focused on the congregation as a whole in pursuing the congregation determined direction and outcomes.

Chapter 11
Operating Policies

The congregation has revised the constitution and bylaws, created the Lay Leadership Group, and authorized the Lay Leadership Group to create the structure needed to carry out the ministry. The next part of the transition process is to understand how to proceed.

One of the major contributions in John Carver's book *Boards That Make a Difference* (ISBN 1-55542-231-4) is an explanation of the importance, construction, and use of operating policies. Some Lay Leadership Groups will want to study the full text.

Carver makes a strong case that each leadership group of a volunteer organization create its own Policy Manual. This process goes a long way toward assuring that the group will understand both the specific policies and the underlying philosophy. We agree with Carver's recommendation.

At the same time, it is also true that many Lay Leadership Groups will not have sufficient time to become trained in the Carver philosophy before starting the new structure. We have also witnessed a habit of some Lay Leadership Groups to create a Policy Manual that is more complex than needed. Some are even more cumbersome than the bylaws they replace.

Appendix E contains a draft Policy Manual for the Lay Leadership Group. This draft gives the Group a solid start. As time passes, additional policies may be needed. Discussions with other churches will uncover useful policies that can be added.

The appendix also has an example of a policy manual for all other boards, committees, action teams, task forces and assorted groups conducting the ministry of the congregation.

Keeping this book open to Appendix E while reading Chapter 11 will aid in understanding the discussion in this chapter.

Lay Leadership Group Policy Manual

The draft Policy Manual contains the minimum content of the four types of policies recommended by Carver. At an early meeting, the newly elected Lay Leadership Group can consider, modify, and adopt the draft. It will give them a good place to start. Changes can be made as issues arise showing the need for improvements in the document.

The Policy Manual is a listing of the conditions under which everyone conducts the church's ministry. Although the text limits what individuals or groups can do, the manual is a permission-giving document and not a list of rules. It is much like the Ten Commandments, which only list the few behaviors that are prohibited. No attempt is made to list what people are permitted to do.

Section A of the draft Policy Manual is normally the fourth type of policy in a typical Carver manual. There are two reasons for listing them first in the draft model. First, these policies guide the overall ministry of the congregation. Second, they should be discussed and approved by the total congregation (Voters' Assembly).

The following comments explain the philosophy and content of each section of the Draft Policy Manual. Readers will want to follow along in Appendix E.

A. Desired Outcomes Policies – Introduction

The opening paragraph summarizes the reason that the congregation exists. Sometimes the paragraph is taken directly from the church's constitution or the church's mission statement. It is a more complete explanation of the congregation's understanding of its overall ministry.

The final words of the introduction might be a slogan or rallying phrase. The phrase should be compelling enough that it does not need to be memorized. It appears in print and orally as often as possible throughout the church. Ideally, everyone would be able to recite it automatically. As such, it should generally not be more than seven words. The way to know if the phrase will be effective is that it is not necessary to spend time memorizing it.

Ministry outcomes are important to new structure. The adage is certainly true that, "If you don't know where you are going, any direction will get you there." Most churches have no idea where they are going. Therefore, any collection of random activities are perceived as achieving the congregation's ministry.

A church and Lay Leadership Group that cares about its ministry are willing to be more focused. A helpful way of proceeding is to create a short, focused, and helpful list of outcomes used to judge how effectively the church's mission is being accomplished.

Ministry outcomes provide a target for the entire church and a focus for the contribution of each board, committee, task force, action team, and most ministries. They provide a standard against which the Lay Leadership Group can judge the fit of all activities with each other. This assessment also helps the Lay Leadership Group understand where within the overall ministry important possibilities may exist.

Each church and Lay Leadership Group needs to create its own list of ministry outcomes. The draft offers some useful examples.

Creating ministry outcomes gives the Lay Leadership Group its meeting agenda (after the initial structural decisions described in Chapter 9). It also helps the Group stay focused on its primary responsibility.

The Lay Leadership Group does not deal with activities. It deals with policies. It interprets policies in the form of outcomes for the entire congregation. (The congregation develops and approves these outcomes.) Programs, boards, committees, task forces, action teams, and the membership all have a part in achieving the outcomes chosen by the congregation.

There are two types of ministry outcomes for the congregation as a whole (and, therefore, the Lay Leadership Group). Primary Ministry Outcomes are those that demonstrate the Great Commission outreach of the church. Secondary Ministry Outcomes are internal to the congregation.

For many churches the provided examples will seem to be placed in the opposite grouping. They are not. The problem is that most churches are accustomed to the churched culture, when taking care of members was the most important aspect of ministry. In the current unchurched culture, thriving congregations have discovered that an extremely powerful way to help members grow spiritually is to focus on outreach.

Primary Ministry Outcomes

The first two ministry outcomes are recommended for all congregations. They come from the insights of Kennon Callahan, as described in *Twelve Keys to an Effective Church* (ISBN 0-7879-3871-8) and several of his other books.

"Persons served in mission" are neither members nor constituents. They are persons in the community who receive direct help from the congregation. Persons served in mission specifically identify the congregation as providing help for some human hurt or hope. Some examples of important ministries that should be continued but are **not** included in the count of persons served in mission are a community food pantry, joint ministry with other churches, and services provided by members but not identified as from the church. Also excluded are activities where the church rents or lends rooms or property to another organization.

Some examples of activities that are included in the count of persons served in mission are:
1. Non-member parents of the preschool operated by the church.
2. Nursing home residents regularly visited by the youth as a group from the church.

3. People receiving emergency food, clothing, or money from the ministry operated at the church.

"Constituents" participate in church activities two or more times in a six-month period, but are not members.

"Change in average weekly worship attendance" is a quick means of assessing the life, health, strength, and vitality. Often persons served in mission will become constituents and later transition to being regular attenders or members.

The "Involvement Ratio" is calculated by dividing the number of the church's "persons serving in a ministry" by "average worship attendance." It is a new concept developed by large churches and recognizes that size is not a primary issue in ministry.

The Involvement Ratio is important, helpful, and difficult to increase. The reason it is hard to increase is that as the church becomes more effective at helping people find their way into ministry, more people are often drawn into the ministry. As the numerator grows, so will the denominator.

The Involvement Ratio will be on the agenda of every board, committee, task force, action team, and all others. There is no reason for any of the aspects of the church's ministry to restrict itself to current participants. As such, every group can be active in increasing the Involvement Ratio.

The fifth line simply indicates that one, two, or three additional Primary Ministry Outcomes can be added. The congregation and Lay Leadership Group are cautioned not to have more than five or six. Churches new to this approach will have fewer. Listing too many outcomes creates unachievable targets and virtually guarantees failure. Smaller congregations coming out of a period of intense internal focus are better helped by limiting themselves to only a few Primary Ministry Outcomes.

Secondary Ministry Outcomes

These are internally focused measures left over from the days of the churched culture. They are helpful in that they can (though not always will) support achievement of the Primary Ministry Outcomes.

Interestingly, one of the most effective ways to achieve the secondary outcomes is to achieve the primary outcomes. All these outcomes support each other, just as all of the church's ministry activities should support each other.

B. Lay Leadership Group Self-Governance Policies

Self-Governance Policies provide an understanding of how the Group is to function. The Introduction contains three policies that demonstrate how the Lay Leadership Group maintains the focus on the overall ministry and stays out of matters better left to other groups. The Lay Leadership Group is well advised to provide the same level of authority to others, such as creating and delivering the ministry area for which they are responsible.

The draft list of "Member Policies" should be carefully examined. The Lay Leadership Group is encouraged to avoid the common practice of speaking platitudes, but not living them out. For example, if the group includes statements calling for participation in education and Bible study, they should also be willing to report attendance. The Lay Leadership Group might then have to face the situation of a Group member who is not willing to actively participate in education and Bible study.

The "Meeting Policies" describe how to conduct the meetings. The statement about Robert's Rules of Order is included only to provide an established procedure during times of stress. The suggested agenda takes effect after the initial meetings to create the structure. At first, the listed agenda will seem awkward. Give it a try and make adjustments as experience is gained.

C. Lay Leadership Group and Senior Pastor Relations

The final set of policies governs the working relationship between the Lay Leadership Group and the Senior Pastor. There are two overarching principles. First, the Lay Leadership Group only operates as whole, with no authority held by any individual member of the group. Second, the Lay

Leadership Group functions with staff exclusively through the Senior Pastor, never giving assignments to other personnel.

These two principles may require some adjustment of thinking among members of the Lay Leadership Group. Many are accustomed to giving ministry instructions to staff and others because of their membership in a group of elected lay leaders. The principle that must be upheld is that nobody is accountable to more than one person or group.

Interestingly, these two principles may also require adjustment in the thinking of the Senior Pastor. Some clergy currently in an equivalent role have difficulty making and being responsible for decisions. The result is that the pastor will consume the limited time of the Lay Leadership Group with minor issues and prevent the group from concentrating on the important overall ministry issues.

D. Senior Pastor
   ### Limitations Policy

The model in Appendix E presents a list that would be used at large churches with multiple staff. The Lay Leadership Group should be realistic about what is really needed and what can be eliminated from the list.

The more important point is that the Senior Pastor is authorized to take any actions not expressly prohibited in the policy. From time to time significant matters may arise that were not considered when creating the policy. In such situations and if time permits, the Senior Pastor is well advised to discuss the issue with the Lay Leadership Group before taking action.

Policies for Boards, Committees, Teams and Other Groups

Appendix E also provides a draft of a policy manual for boards and committees. In order to simplify the discussion, the draft in Appendix E only refers to the Education Ministry. However, variation of these policies also applies to every board, committee, task force, action team, and other group.

This document is a balance between being helpful to the mission of the congregation and being so burdensome that it would not be used. Consequently, the draft is kept short and easy to use.

While much of the draft suggests large amounts of self-determination, one component about the congregation's overall structure is of critical importance. The Lay Leadership Group has been authorized by the congregation to create and recreate the structure whereby the church conducts ministry. Thus, in those rare instances where one ministry goes considerably outside the church's direction, the Lay Leadership Group possesses the ultimate authority to make changes.

A. Desired Outcomes

The first page of the draft policy is new to virtually all congregations. The first section of the first page restates the central mission of the church, and then focuses that mission to the activities of the Education Ministry.

For the Education Ministry leaders to think of their activities specifically in the context of the congregation's mission is a significant departure from the churched culture days when merely being busy was considered appropriate. If developing a few lines of text linking the Ministry with the overall congregation is difficult for the Education Ministry, then that ministry is probably engaged in activities not supportive to the overall mission of the church.

The remainder of the first page asks the Education Ministry to select targets for primary and secondary ministry outcomes that are parallel to the overall mission of the church. This will be a significant challenge for the Education Ministry and most others. Creating these ministry outcome targets is critical in three ways:

1. It focuses for the Education Ministry their importance to the church's overall ministry.
2. When combined with similar outcome targets for all other groups, it gives the Lay Leadership Group better information with which to judge the likelihood of the church achieving its Voter-selected ministry goals.

3. Annually reviewing levels of achievement helps the Education Ministry and the Lay Leadership Group assess whether the Education Ministry is contributing to the church's overall ministry or simply conducting a series of activities for sake of the activities.

The selected ministry outcomes can be of many types. Some will lend themselves to being counted and others will not. The important point is to be specific about outcomes as an aid to focusing the efforts of the staff and/or volunteers conducting the ministry.

The remainder of the Education Ministry policies will be easy and includes several recommendations that will be favorably received.

B. Primary Activities

The next section is a listing of the Education Ministry's primary activities. This listing of the major activities in one or more specific areas will be easy for the Education Ministry and helpful for the church's leaders. New ideas being tested or simply discussed can also be included.

C. Education Ministry Policies

The Education Ministry Policies begin with a simple listing of their "Duties." This listing describes their linkage with the overall leadership of the church.

The "Membership" subsection lists the size of the board. Determining the size should probably be left to the discretion of the Education Ministry and concurred with by the Lay Leadership Group. In keeping with prior discussion, the draft suggests that there not be any term limits for Education Ministry Board membership.

Perhaps the newest concept for the Education Ministry (and the Lay Leadership Group) is contained in the third point under "Membership." The draft recommends that the Education Ministry Board determine how to select people for membership on the board. It can decide the pool from which to choose membership (e.g. Voters in general, parents of participants in the programs, etc.). Removing this task from the Lay Leadership Group and the congregation's Nomi-

nating Committee will be welcomed by all concerned.

D. Board and Staff Relations

The final portion of the Education Ministry's policies describes the relationship between that board and the paid or volunteer staff. There will be wide variation in this section, depending upon the complexity of the paid and non-paid staffing patterns.

The main point to be maintained in drafting wording for this section is that no one reports to more than one entity. Paid staff will most likely report to the Senior Pastor. As such, the Education Ministry Board acts in an advisory capacity. If there is a volunteer leader, then a choice is needed between reporting to the board or to the Senior Pastor—but not both.

The drafts of the Lay Leadership Group Policy Manual and the example Education Ministry Policies give the church's leadership a good start in creating documents that aid the congregation in achieving the ministry selected by the Voters. As time is available, study of the books by Carver and Callahan will assist the leaders in understanding where and how to apply the leadership entrusted to them by the congregation.

Chapter 12
Spiritual/Ministry Development

Chapter 12 provides an overview discussion of a very large topic. Several terms have been used in recent years to describe the concept. Each of these terms carries a somewhat different nuance and corresponding set of activities. We prefer the first listed term:

- Spiritual development
- Lay mobilization
- Equipping ministry
- Spiritual gifts
- Ministry development

In one sense this is a new topic which, given its size, perhaps has no place in this book about constitutions and bylaws. In a larger sense, spiritual development is the primary reason for adopting a flexible, missional document.

Most congregations undertake rewriting their constitution and bylaws because of growing difficulties with structure, volunteer recruitment, or simply "getting things done." Those certainly are good reasons for making the transition.

We hope that the discussion in Chapters 2, 3, and 4 left the clear understanding that the approach suggested in the book is grounded in a desire to expand the number of people involved in ministry. Indeed, eliminating the barriers that prevent participation is motivated by the desire to expand ministry involvement, and not a lesser goal of easing the burden on current leaders.

The reason for expanding ministry involvement is to help more people achieve higher levels of spiritual development. Size and growth are natural outcomes that sometimes accompany spiritual development, but size and growth are not the objectives.

Indeed, most congregations experiencing success in Great Commission ministry explain that spiritual development is the goal, not numerical size or growth. They have found that spiritual development happens when people are actively and personally involved in ministry activity. Consequently, these churches focus on helping individuals find their way into a ministry that best fits their God-given gifts and passions.

Congregations that adopt a new constitution without also considering spiritual development will achieve only partial success. Progress will be made, but God's mission will be limited.

Spiritual development is fostered when at least two types of systems are well in place. The first helps individuals identify a meaningful ministry, and the second provides a mechanism through which the congregation provides a way for people to become involved in ministry.

Identifying a meaningful ministry

Many different instruments are available to help people identify a way to express themselves in ministry. They are widely known and can be found in most catalogs of religious materials or through denominational judicatory personnel who help churches.

We use and recommend *LifeKeys* by Jane Kise, David Stark, and Sandra Hirsh. A full set of materials is published by Bethany House Publishers of Minneapolis, Minnesota (800-991-7747 or www.BethanyHouse.com). The materials include a textbook, leaders guide, and participant workbook.

The LifeKeys process helps participants assess themselves in seven key areas of life.

1. God has an important mission for everyone.

   The first LifeKey is a general, simple, and biblical concept containing three parts:

- Each human being is created in the image of God (Genesis 1:26-27).
- All are created with a unique, specifically chosen blend of gifts (Psalm 139:13-16).
- God has in mind specific good works for each person to accomplish (Ephesians 2:10).

2. **Life Gifts.** Doing what comes naturally is part of God's plan. Some are more comfortable being realistic, investigative, artistic, social, enterprising, or conventional. Everyone has some level of life gift in more than one area.

3. **Spiritual Gifts.** Everyone has one or more spiritual gifts. Some examples are helping, hospitality, giving, evangelism, teaching, wisdom, and fourteen additional gifts used in the LifeKeys materials.

4. **Personality Type.** Personality typology is identified using an abbreviated version of Myers-Briggs to help people differentiate between extroversion or introversion, sensing or intuition, thinking or feeling, and judging or perceiving.

5. **Values.** The materials help individuals prioritize their values, from a list of fifty-one options (e.g., accuracy, balance, fairness, family, humor, etc.).

6. **Passions.** Passion is what brings people joy. These are things one really feels called to do. Once in a while the participant is already doing them, but often that is not the case.

7. **Life Choices.** The final life choice is to select which of five Biblical principles mean the most to doing the self-assessment. The principles are:
- Put first things first—seek the Kingdom of God
- Know your mission
- Know your limits
- Simplify—aim for balance in your life
- Reflect on people who seem to "have enough time"

Completing a LifeKeys assessment helps everyone find a ministry outlet. Sometimes that outlet matches current activities, but often it does not.

Helping people find ministry outlets is critical to achieving the congregation's mission goals using a flexible, missional constitution and bylaws. The congregation needs an individual at the church to become skilled in whatever approach is used. That person (or group) then helps all those participating with the church to identify a ministry area.

Completing the individual assessment can be accomplished in a variety of ways. Some are:
- Using the normal Bible study time for several weeks
- Conducting a major weekend event
- Holding classes or gatherings over a period of several weeks
- Completing the assessment in new member classes
- Using a portion of several meetings of the Lay Leadership Group
- Holding an all-congregation leadership retreat

Helping people identify their ministry gifts is critical. Churched culture structures are motivated to fill slots on the mandated boards and committees. Mission outpost congregations are eager to help people find a fulfilling ministry. The important point is to help people achieve spiritual growth through direct, personal involvement in ministry.

Mechanism for involvement in ministry

Once people identify a ministry that will be personally meaningful, the other important aspect of implementing a flexible, missional constitution and bylaws is having in place a mechanism to make that happen. Mechanisms are available for churches to become effective in helping individuals find a ministry outlet.

Before discussing exactly how that can happen, there is one important point. Sometimes the specific ministry selected by the individual is outside the ministry of the congregation. Mission-driven churches do not hoard ministry gifts. They are entirely comfortable helping people find their way to ministry outlets. Remember, size and growth of the congregation are not the issue. The issue is helping people grow spiritually.

We also need to mention one common system that should generally be abandoned. It is commonly called the "Time and Talent" sheet. This is a listing of all boards, committees, and programs of the church that need volunteers. Members, particularly new members, are asked to check those activities in which they might be interested.

"Time and Talent" surveys have at least two problems. The first is that they are rarely used. Virtually everyone who completes a "Time and Talent" sheet never hears from anyone. This common reality is particularly troubling to new members. They work hard to accurately complete the form, hear nothing, and conclude that they are not needed or perhaps not even wanted. This almost universal reality is a "bucket of cold water" on an otherwise enthused new member. In most instances, "Time and Talent" surveys have become a most effective rejection system.

The other problem with "Time and Talent" sheets is more to the point of this book. They are focused on the needs of the congregation. As such they miss most of the ministry outlet needs of the members, new members, future members, participants who are not members, and virtually anyone who could support the ministry of the congregation.

A more helpful approach is a formal system to help people identify a ministry, find a ministry, and carry out a ministry. A number of these congregational systems are available. Here again, they are widely available from distributors of religious materials and from denominational judicatory personnel.

We recommend the Equipping Ministry materials and methods from the Leadership Training Network of Dallas, Texas (877-586-5323 or www.LTN.org). Guidebooks and training at one-day, two-day, and week-long sessions are available.

The model developed by Leadership Training Network has seven components:

1. **Assimilation**. Learning what the church is and how to become a part of it
2. **Context**. Understanding the biblical context for gifts and ministry involvement
3. **Discovery**. Identifying the unique set of gifts and interests
4. **Matching**. Identifying the ways those gifts and interests can be used in ministry
5. **Placement**. Making contact with the ministry area
6. **Coaching**. Receiving training and encouragement in the ministry area
7. **Recognition**. Celebrating the ministry, exit interviews, and new placement

The Leadership Training Network materials are extremely complete. A full-time Director of Equipping Ministries can use them as an operational manual. A part-time paid or volunteer staff member can use parts of the total system.

Congregations seeking a way out of the straitjacket of a complex and rigid constitution and bylaws created in times of the churched culture will experience ministry release by adopting a flexible, missional structure. Ministry will be greatly aided by this transition alone. This book has explained how to create that new document in one day, not the normal two or more years.

Great Commission ministry growth lies in focusing on spiritual development of those leading and participating in the ministry. The last chapter of this book seeks to encourage the church leaders' understanding that putting a flexible, missional constitution in place is an excellent start. Pursuing the twin activities of identifying meaningful ministry and creating a mechanism to make it happen are important to following through on the goal of becoming a mission outpost on the church's local mission field.

Appendix A
Constitution and Bylaws of
St. Paul Church

ST. PAUL CHURCH
CONSTITUTION

PREAMBLE

The Word of God demands that a Christian congregation not only conform to the Word of God in doctrine and practice (Psalm 119:105, Galatians 1:6-8). It also states that all things be done decently and in order (I Corinthians 14:40). Therefore, we the members of St. Paul Church, set forth this constitution and bylaws to govern all our congregational affairs.

ARTICLE I: NAME

The name of this congregation shall be St. Paul Church.

ARTICLE II: STATEMENT OF MISSION

To reach out and bring people into a living relationship with Jesus Christ through dynamic worship of God, vigorous study of His Word, loving care for one another and committed support of His work throughout the world.

ARTICLE III: CONFESSIONAL STANDARD

This congregation accepts all the Canonical Books of the Old and New Testaments as the revealed Word of God, verbally inspired; and it accepts all the three Ecumenical Creeds (Apostles, Nicene and Athanasian), the Unaltered Augsburg Confession, the Apology of the Augsburg Confession, the Smalcald Articles, Catechism and the Formula of Concord. All preaching and teaching must be in accord with the above, and all doctrinal controversies which may occur shall be decided in accordance with the same.

ARTICLE IV: DENOMINATIONAL AFFILIATION

This congregation with its pastor(s) and called teacher(s) shall be a members of the Denomination so long as said denomination shall remain true to the confessional standard as set forth in Article III of this constitution.

ARTICLE V: MEMBERSHIP

The membership of this congregation includes baptized, confirmed and voting members. The admission of new members and termination of membership shall be set forth in policies established by the Board of Directors in accordance with the spirit of this constitution. The types and duties of membership are as follows:

A. Baptized Members - Baptized members are all persons within the congregation who have been baptized in the name of the Triune God, whether children or adults, and come under the pastoral care of this congregation. It is expected of all baptized members that they:
1. Attend worship services faithfully and regularly;
2. Lead a Christian life as taught in Galatians 5:19-26;
3. Out of Christian love, submit to brotherly admonition, according to Matthew 18, when having erred or offended;
4. Contribute, as God has blessed them, of their time, talents and treasure toward the maintenance of the congregation and the extension of the church at large;
5. In due time, take a course of instruction in preparation for confirmed membership in this congregation;
6. Are not members of any organization conflicting with the Word of God.

B. Confirmed Members - Confirmed members are all baptized persons within the congregation who have received a course of instruction in Christian doctrine which meets with the approval of the Board of Directors. In addition to the duties of baptized members, it is expected of all confirmed members that they:
1. Accept all Canonical Books of the Old and New Testament as the standard of faith and life;
2. Familiarize themselves with the doctrines of this church, at least as set forth in the Catechism and declare acceptance of them;
3. Partake of the Lord's Supper at least one time per calendar year;
4. Provide for the Christian training of their children by making use of the educational agencies of the church;
5. Submit willingly and cheerfully to the policies already made or still to be made, provided such policies do not conflict with the Word of God.

C. Voting Members - Voting membership shall be confirmed members in accordance with this constitution who have attained the age of 18 years. It is expected of all voting members that they shall:
1. Attend all meetings of the Voters' Assembly faithfully;
2. Serve faithfully, according to their God-given talents, in any capacity in which they may be called upon to serve.

ARTICLE VI: THE OFFICES OF PASTOR AND TEACHER
The pastoral office of this congregation as well as that of a called teacher in the Christian Day School shall be conferred upon only such ministers, teachers and candidates as profess and adhere to the confessional standards set forth in Article III of this constitution and who are well qualified for their work. Pastor and teachers shall, in the call wended to and accepted by them, be pledged to this confessional standard.

ARTICLE VII: POWERS OF THE CONGREGATION
A. General - The congregation as a body, through its Voters' Assembly, shall have supreme power to administer and manage all of the congregation's external and internal affairs. The congregation, however, shall not be empowered to decide anything contrary to the Word of God and the confessions listed in Article III, and any such contrary decision shall be null and void. Matters of doctrine and conscience shall be decided in accordance with the Word of God. Other matters shall be decided by a simple majority vote of the voting members in attendance at a Voters' Assembly meeting unless otherwise specified by this constitution or bylaws.
B. Right of Calling - The right of calling pastors and other called workers shall be vested in the Voters' Assembly and shall not be delegated to a smaller body or an individual. The Board of Directors may authorize the hiring of non-called staff as approved in the annual budget or by the Voters' Assembly.
C. Election of Officers and the Board of Directors - The Voters' Assembly shall elect a Chairman, Vice-Chairman, Secretary, and Treasurer. These individuals shall be the officers of the congregation. The Voters' Assembly shall also elect seven (7) other voting members. These seven (7) members plus the four (4) officers and the Senior Pastor shall comprise the Board of Directors. The Senior Pastor shall be a non-voting member of the Board. The nomination and election of officers and Board members shall be as specified in the bylaws.
D, Board of Directors Actions Requiring, Prior Approval of the Voters' Assembly - The Board of Directors shall obtain prior approval of the Voters' Assembly on the following actions/items.
  1. Annual Financial Operating Plan
  2. Acquisition or disposal of any single asset or liability that exceeds 1% of the annual operating budget
  3. Calling or removal of called staff
  4. Dissolution of the congregation
E. Removal from Office - Any pastor, other called worker, officer or board member, who fails to perform the duties of confirmed members as stated in Article V, or is unable or is willfully neglectful in the performance of his official duties, may be removed from office in Christian and lawful order by the Voters' Assembly. Such action shall be initiated through a member of the Board of Directors.

ARTICLE VIII: POWERS OF THE BOARD OF DIRECTORS
A. Officers and Executive Committee - The officers of the congregation shall also serve as the Executive Committee. The Executive Committee will obtain its power and authority for action at the express designation of the full Board. The Chairman and Secretary shall sign all legal documents.
B. Board of Directors - The Board of Directors shall have the power to develop and implement those policies and procedures as required to execute the plans approved by the Voters' Assembly. Written policies and procedures shall be available to voting members upon request. The Board shall have no authority beyond that which has been conferred upon them by the constitution, its bylaws or by the Voters' Assembly, and powers delegated to them may at any time be altered or revoked by the Voters' Assembly.
C. Duties of the Board
  1. The Board shall assist the Pastor(s) in all matters pertaining to the spiritual welfare of the congregation.
  2. The Board shall watch over the doctrine, life, and administration of the office of the Pastor(s) and called staff. The Board shall monitor the welfare of the Pastor(s), called and administration staff, and provide pastoral care as appropriate. The Board shall supervise the Senior Pastor and ensure proper supervision of the staff. Such supervision shall enable the staff to develop and implement new strategies and programs to accomplish the mission as stated in Article II.
  3. The Board shall transact or supervise the transaction of all legal and general business of the congregation.
  4. The Board shall conduct business within the limitations of the annual financial operating plan approved by the Voters' Assembly.
  5. The Board shall annually report to the Voters' Assembly on the organizational and financial condition of the congregation. It shall also recommend an annual financial operating plan at the annual Voters' Assembly meeting.

ARTICLE IX: PROPERTY RIGHTS

All property of this congregation shall be held in the corporate name as stated in Article I. If at any time a separation should take place in this congregation, the property of the congregation and all benefits pertaining thereto shall remain with those members who shall continue to adhere to Article III and Article IV of this constitution. In the event of the dissolution of this congregation, all property of the congregation shall be disposed of by the final Voters' Assembly for the payment of debts, and any and all surplus, after due settlement of just claims against this congregation, shall be conveyed to and become the property of the judicatory of the Denomination to which the church belongs.

ARTICLE X: BYLAWS

This congregation, through its Voters' Assembly, may adopt such bylaws as the accomplishment of the purpose of this organization may demand.

ARTICLE XI: AMENDMENTS

A. Amendments - Amendments to this Constitution may be proposed in writing in any Voters' Assembly meeting by any voting member. If the majority of the voting members present shall vote in favor of the proposal a copy of such proposed amendment shall be mailed to all voting members at least two (2) weeks preceding the next meeting. Thereupon the final vote shall be taken in that meeting, or at a duly publicized continuation of that meeting, and a two-thirds (2/3) majority of the voting members there present shall be required for adoption. Upon adoption, such amendment shall be submitted to the Judicatory Committee on Constitutions for approval in accordance with the Denomination's Bylaws.

B. Unalterable Articles - The following articles of this Constitution or sections thereof shall be unalterable and irreplaceable: Article III (Confessional Standard); Article VI (The Offices of Pastor and Teacher); and this Article XIB.

BYLAWS

ARTICLE 1: VOTERS' ASSEMBLY

1. Meetings - The Voters' Assembly shall meet at least annually. The day and hour of the annual meeting shall be set by the Board of Directors and publicized at least two weeks in advance. The notification shall contain an agenda of items to be considered as well as the slate of nominees for election. The Voters' Assembly may meet at other times of the year subject to a call by the Board of Directors, or at the request of any twelve (12) voting members. Notice of any such special meeting shall be publicized as far in advance as possible but no less than one week in advance. The notice shall contain an agenda of items to be considered. No agenda items may be added once notification of any meeting is publicized. The Chair, Vice Chair, or their designated Board member shall preside at all Voters' Assembly meetings.

2. Quorum - A quorum of fifty (50) of the voting membership must be present to conduct the business of the Voters' Assembly.

ARTICLE 2: BOARD OF DIRECTORS

1. Nominating Committee- The Vice Chairman of the Board shall annually appoint a Nominating Committee whose responsibility will be to develop a slate of officers and Board members to be elected each year to fill the vacancies created by expired terms of officers and board members. The committee shall contain a majority of non-board members, shall function for one year only, and shall report their nominations to the Voters' Assembly annual meeting. The Senior Pastor shall be a non-voting member of the Nominating Committee. All nominees shall be voting members.

2. Elections and Terms of Office - The members of the Board of Directors shall be elected by the Voters' Assembly. The term of office shall be for a maximum of two years, with approximately one half of the Board being elected each year. Board members shall serve no more than two full successive terms. Immediately following the election of the new Board members, the Voters' Assembly shall elect a Chairman, Vice Chairman, Secretary and Treasurer from the members of the Board. These officers shall be elected for a one-year term. Every term of office shall begin on January I following the election. In the event of a vacancy on the Board of Directors, the Nominating Committee shall provide the Chairman with a list of candidates. Appointments to fill unexpired terms will be made from such list and must be ratified by a majority vote of the Board. The individual shall serve until the next election for that particular position. In addition to the Nominating Committee's slate of candidates, any voting member may nominate any other Board positions. Such nominations shall be called for in the annual Voters' Assembly meeting prior to the time that nominations are closed.

3. <u>Meetings</u> - The Board of Directors shall meet at least quarterly and may be called more frequently at the request of the Chairman or any three Board members. Seven (7) members of the Board of Directors shall constitute a quorum for any meeting. Minutes of each meeting shall be kept in typed form. The minutes shall fully disclose all actions taken and be signed by the Chairman and Secretary. Minutes of the meetings shall be available to voting members upon request.

ARTICLE 3: DUTIES OF OFFICERS

A. <u>Chairman</u> - The duties of the Chairman shall be as follows:
1. Preside at all meetings of the Voters' Assembly and the Board of Directors.
2. Serve as a non-voting member of all committees.
3. Appoint any necessary committees.
4. Sign all legal documents, with the Secretary, on behalf of the congregation.
5. Enforce the constitution and bylaws and perform the general duties as are common for the office, including such additional duties as may be directed by the Voters' Assembly from time to time.

B. <u>Vice-Chairman</u> - The duties of the Vice-Chairman shall be as follows:
1. Perform all of the duties of the Chairman in the latter's absence and such other additional duties which may be directed by the Voters' Assembly or by the Chairman from time to time.
2. Chair and appoint a Nominating Committee with the advice and consent of the Board of Directors.

C. <u>Secretary</u> - The duties of the Secretary shall be as follows:
1. The duties shall be those commonly required of that office, especially the keeping and preserving of accurate records of all Voters' Assembly meetings, and handling such correspondence as the congregation may require.
2. Sign all legal documents, with the Chairman, on behalf of the congregation.
3. Keep minutes of all Board of Directors meetings.

D. <u>Treasurer</u> - The duties of the Treasurer shall be as follows:
1. Keep and preserve the accurate records of all receipts and disbursements, and submit a written report of them at all regular meetings of the Voters' Assembly.
2. Pay all regular and fixed expenses on order of the Voters! Assembly.

ARTICLE 4: AMENDMENTS

Amendments to these Bylaws may be made in the following manner:

A copy of the proposed amendment shall be mailed to all voting members at least two (2) weeks prior to a Voters' Assembly meeting. At this meeting the vote shall be taken on the amendment and two-thirds (2/3) of the voting members present shall secure adoption. Upon adoption, such amendments shall be submitted to the District Committee on Constitutions for approval, in accordance with the Denomination's Bylaws.

Appendix B
Draft Constitution and Bylaws

Draft Constitution of
First Church
City, State

Preamble

It is the will of our Lord Jesus Christ that His disciples should preach the gospel to the whole world (Mark 16:16, Matthew 23:18-20, Acts 1:8). Therefore we have organized to be a mission outpost which deliberately seeks to connect broken lives to a healing Jesus through education, dynamic worship, and significant relational groups.

Article I
Name

The name of this congregation shall be First Church of City, State.

Article II
Purpose

The purposes for which this congregation is formed, in addition to those stated in the Articles of Incorporation, are:
A. To establish and maintain the Office of the Christian Ministry in our midst.
B. To facilitate spreading the Christian faith in our community and around the world.
C. To establish and maintain Christian education and training of youth and adults.
D. To foster Christian fellowship and charity.
E. To acquire, hold title to, sell, transfer, convey and otherwise dispose of property-real, personal, and mixed.

Article III
Confession of Faith

Enter the congregation/denomination standards of faith.

Article IV
Denominational Affiliation

This congregation shall be affiliated with the *Denomination* as long as the confessions and constitution of the *Denomination* are in accord with the confessions and constitution of this congregation as laid down in Article III.

Article V
Membership

The membership of this congregation includes the Baptized Members, Communicant Members, and Voting Members as defined in the bylaws.

Article VI
Organization

A. Voters' Assembly
The Voters' Assembly shall consist of all voting members present at a regular or special meeting of the congregation. The congregation, through the Voters' Assembly, shall have final authority in managing its internal and external affairs.

B. Lay Leadership Group
The Lay Leadership Group shall be the governing body of the congregation and is responsible to administer all the congregation's affairs except the following matters for action only by the Voters' Assembly:
   1. Call or remove a called worker.
   2. Purchase or sell church property or buildings valued over 10% of the annual operating budget.
   3. Incur a non-budgeted emergency expense of over 5% of the annual expense budget of the congregation.
   4. Adopt the Annual Financial Plan.
   5. Dissolve the congregation.

C. Officers and Boards
The officers of this congregation shall be such officers as the bylaws of this constitution prescribe. The officers and boards prescribed in the bylaws shall have no authority beyond that which has been conferred upon them in the constitution or bylaws.

Article VII
Property Rights

A. Division within the congregation
If, at any time, a separation shall take place within this congregation, the advice of the officers of the denomination shall be sought. If, despite all efforts to resolve differences in peace and love, a division into factions of the congregation shall occur, the property of the congregation and all benefits connected shall remain with (**the majority** or **the faction selected by the denomination**).

B. Dissolution of the congregation
If the congregation is dissolved, after settling all debts, the remaining assets shall be transferred **to the denomination**.

Article VIII
Decisions

All congregational matters decided by the Voters' Assembly shall be decided by a simple majority of the voting members present at a properly convened meeting of the Voters' Assembly, except as otherwise provided in this constitution and bylaws. Procedural questions will be decided by following *Robert's Rules of Order*.

Article IX
Amendments

This constitution may be amended by a two-thirds majority of the votes cast in a meeting of the Voters' Assembly. The wording of the amended constitution and bylaws shall be distributed to all members in a mailing as far in advance as possible, but no fewer than two Sundays in advance. In addition, the revisions will be distributed to the congregation assembled for worship on two different Sundays prior to the date upon which the amendment is presented for action.

Bylaws of
First Church
City, State

Article 1
Baptized Membership

Baptized members are all persons within the congregation who have been baptized in the name of the Triune God and come under the pastoral care of this congregation. It is expected that all baptized members will:
A. Attend worship services faithfully and regularly.
B. Lead a Christian life as taught in Galatians 5:19-26.
C. Out of Christian love, submit to brotherly admonition, according to Matthew 18, when having erred or offended.
D. Contribute, as God has blessed them, of their time, talents and treasure toward the maintenance of the congregation and the extension of the church at large.
E. In due time, take a course of instruction in preparation for confirmed membership in this congregation.

Article 2
Confirmed Membership

Confirmed members are all baptized persons within the congregation who have completed a course of instruction in Christian doctrine that meets with the approval of the Lay Leadership Group.

Persons seeking to attain confirmed membership shall make that fact known to the Senior Pastor or any other delegated pastor. The pastor shall ascertain the understanding and commitment to the purpose and theological commitment contained in Article III. The pastor will determine if additional training is needed and the appropriate method for that training. The pastor is authorized to extend confirmed membership to the person and shall announce that in a public service.

In addition to the duties of baptized members, it is expected of all confirmed members that they:
A. Accept the confessions of faith listed in Article III of the constitution.
B. Familiarize themselves with the doctrines of the *Denomination*.
C. Partake of the Lord's Supper.
D. Participate in continuing Christian education.
E. Provide for the Christian training of their children by making use of the educational agencies of the congregation.

Article 3
Voting Membership

Voting members are all communicant members who attend a Voters' meeting.

Article 4
Termination of Membership

A. Transfers
   A member desiring transfer to another congregation shall make that fact known to the Senior Pastor. The Senior Pastor shall cause the creating and mailing of a letter of transfer to the receiving congregation.
B. Whereabouts unknown or moved
   The names of members whose whereabouts are unknown or who have moved from the area may be removed from membership after a period of one year.

C. Discipline

All discipline in this congregation shall be administered in accordance with Matthew 18:15-20. The purpose of any disciplinary action is to renew a member's relationship with the Lord and with the church. A member shall be considered self-excluded when unresponsive to the witness and ministry of the church.

Article 5
Voters' Assembly

A. The Voters' Assembly shall meet at least once a year. The day and hour of the annual meeting shall be set by the Lay Leadership Group and publicized at least one month in advance. The notification shall contain an agenda of items to be considered as well as the slate of nominees for election.

B. The Voters' Assembly may meet at other times of the year subject to a call by the Lay Leadership Group or at the request of any _____ voting members of the congregation. Notice of any such special meeting shall be publicized as far in advance as possible but no less than one week in advance. The notice shall contain an agenda of items to be considered. No agenda items may be added once notification of any meeting is publicized. The Chairperson, Vice Chairperson, or their designated Lay Leadership Group member shall preside at all Voters' Assembly meetings.

C. A quorum of _____ voting members must be present to conduct the business of the Voters' Assembly. If a quorum is not present, the chairperson will suspend the meeting for a period of not less that one week. When the meeting is resumed, the quorum shall be all those in attendance at the resumed meeting.

Article 6
Called Workers

A. Called Workers
   1. Calls will only be issued to such candidates who are approved by the *Denomination*.
   2. After authorization is received from the Voters' Assembly, the Lay Leadership Group shall appoint a Call Committee. No more than one-third of the Call Committee members may be members of the Lay Leadership Group.
   3. The Call Committee shall consult with those in the affected ministry area and with the *Denominational Judicatory* as part of their efforts to secure the names of candidates.
   4. The Call Committee will present a final list of candidates to the Voters' Assembly for issuance of the Call.

B. Removal from Office of Called Workers

Any Called Worker may be removed from office by the Voters' Assembly by a three-fourths majority secret ballot vote because of: persistent adherence to false doctrine, scandalous life, neglect of duties, inability to perform the duties of the office, or other significant reason determined by the Voters' Assembly.

Article 7
Officers

A. Chairperson:
   1. Preside at all meetings of the Voters' Assembly and the Lay Leadership Group.
   2. Enforce the constitution and bylaws.
   3. Perform the general duties as are common for the office, including such additional duties as may be directed by the Voters' Assembly from time to time.

B. Vice Chairperson:
   1. Perform all of the duties of the Chairperson in the latter's absence and such other additional duties which may be directed by the Voters' Assembly or by the Chairperson from time to time.
   2. Chair and appoint a Nominating Committee with the advice and consent of the Lay Leadership Group.

C. Secretary:
   1. The duties shall be those commonly required of that office, especially the keeping and preserving of accurate records of all Voters' Assembly meetings, and handling such correspondence as the congregation may require.
   2. Keep and make available minutes of all Lay Leadership Group meetings.

D. Treasurer:
   1. Keep and preserve the accurate records of all receipts and disbursements, and submit a written report of them at all regular meetings of the Voters' Assembly.
   2. Assure accuracy and propriety of all financial transactions of the congregation.
F. Term of Office
   Each officer shall serve for a term of ___ years and shall serve no more than ___ full successive terms in that position without a break of at least ___ year.

Article 8
Lay Leadership Group

A. Membership
   The Lay Leadership Group shall consist of ___ voting members, elected at large by the Voters' Assembly, plus the congregation officers listed in Article 7. The Senior Pastor is a non-voting member.
B. Term of Office
   The term of office shall be ___ years, with approximately ___ of the Lay Leadership Group being elected each year. Group members shall serve no more than ___ full successive terms in that position without a break of at least ___ year.
C. Meetings
   The Lay Leadership Group shall meet at least quarterly and may be called more frequently at the request of the Chairperson or any three Lay Leadership Group members. An elected officer shall be present and preside with ___ members of the Lay Leadership Group to constitute a quorum for any meeting. Notice of each meeting shall be posted. The minutes shall fully disclose all actions taken and be signed by the Chairperson and Secretary. Minutes of the meetings shall be available to voting members upon request.

Article 9
Powers of the Lay Leadership Group

The Lay Leadership Group shall have the power to develop policies as required to execute the goals approved by the Voters' Assembly. Written policies shall be available upon request. The Group shall have no authority beyond that which has been conferred upon them by the constitution, its bylaws, or by the Voters' Assembly.

Article 10
Duties of the Lay Leadership Group

A. The Lay Leadership Group, as the chief governing Council of the congregation, shall act in all matters pertaining to the legal and general welfare of the congregation, except those reserved for the Voters' Assembly in Article VI.B. of the constitution.
B. The Lay Leadership Group shall see to it that all activities of the church reflect the purpose and faith of the congregation.
C. It shall concern itself with establishing all policies governing the activities of the congregation and with the implementation of the mission, vision, budget, and plans adopted by the Voters' Assembly.
D. The Lay Leadership Group may appoint any entity needed. It shall oversee and have authority over all other boards, committees, task forces, action teams, or other entities of the congregation.

Article 11
Election, Removal from Office, and Vacancies

A. Nomination
The Vice Chairperson of the Lay Leadership Group shall annually appoint a Nominating Committee whose responsibility will be to develop a slate of candidates for officers and Lay Leadership Group members to be elected each year. The committee shall contain a majority who are not on the Lay Leadership Group members, shall function for one year only, and shall report their nominations to the election meeting of the Voters' Assembly. The Senior Pastor shall be a non-voting member of the Nominating Committee.

All nominees shall be voting members noted for their Christian knowledge, zeal, and experience in the spiritual work in the Kingdom. Specific criteria for elected officials shall be outlined by the Nominating Committee prior to accepting any nominations. In addition to the Nominating Committee's slate of candidates, any voting member may nominate candidates. A call for nominations will be distributed to the congregation no fewer than two months prior to the election meeting. The list of nominations will be closed at the time that the meeting agenda and slate of candidates is distributed.

Those elected by the voters may not receive compensation from the congregation and may not lead any group that reports directly to the Lay Leadership Group, except a Call Committee or the Nominations Committee.

B. Election
Nominees who receive a majority of the ballots cast at the Voters' Assembly shall be the elected.
C. Taking office
All elected officials will begin their term of office **on the second Sunday of the month following election**.
D. Vacancy
The Lay Leadership Group shall be authorized to appoint a person to fill an unexpired term of an officer.
E. Removal from Office of Elected Officials
Any elected official, who is unable or is willfully neglectful in the performance of his official duties, may be removed from office by two-thirds secret ballot vote of the Voters' Assembly. Such action shall be initiated by the Lay Leadership Group.

Article 12
(Name of Endowment Fund – if present)

The purpose of the *(name of endowment fund)* (a non-profit organization charter under the laws of the State of _____) is to receive and invest funds for the purposes established by the congregation and presented in the *(name the document containing the rules and procedures)*. The Directors of this Foundation shall be communicant members of *name of church*. All rules, regulations, and policies shall be made available upon request to any member of the congregation. The Directors of the Foundation shall provide a report annually to the Voters' Assembly.

Article 13
Amendments

The bylaws may be amended by a two-thirds majority of the votes cast in a meeting of the Voters' Assembly. The wording of the amended constitution and bylaws shall be distributed to all members in a mailing as far in advance as possible, but no fewer that two Sundays in advance. In addition, the revisions will be distributed to the congregation assembled for worship on two different Sundays prior to the date upon which the amendment is presented for action.

Appendix C
Other Wordings of Constitution and Bylaws Sections

Membership   Page 64

Voters   Page 66

Called Workers   Page 68

Officers   Page 70

Lay Leadership Group   Page 72

Membership – Example #1

ARTICLE V: MEMBERSHIP

The membership of this congregation includes baptized, confirmed and voting members. The admission of new members and termination of membership shall be set forth in policies established by the Board of Directors in accordance with the spirit of this constitution. The types and duties of membership are as follows:

A. Baptized Members

Baptized members are all persons within the congregation who have been baptized in the name of the Triune God, whether children or adults, and come under the pastoral care of this congregation. It is expected of all baptized members that they:

1. Attend worship services faithfully and regularly;
2. Lead a Christian life as taught in Galatians 5:19-26;
3. Out of Christian love, submit to brotherly admonition, according to Matthew 18, when having erred or offended;
4. Contribute, as God has blessed them of their time, talents and treasure toward the maintenance of the congregation and the extension of the church at large;
5. In due time, take a course of instruction in preparation for confirmed membership in this congregation;
6. Are not members of any organization conflicting with the Word of God.

B. Confirmed Members

Confirmed members are all baptized persons within the congregation who have received a course of instruction in Christian doctrine which meets with the approval of the Board of Directors. In addition to the duties of baptized members, it is expected of all confirmed members that they:

1. Accept all Canonical Books of the Old and New Testament as the only divine rule and standard of faith and life;
2. Familiarize themselves with the doctrines of the Church, at least as set forth in the Catechism and declare acceptance of them;
3. Partake of the Lord's Supper at least one time per calendar year;
4. Provide for the Christian training of their children by making use of the educational agencies of the congregation;
5. Submit willingly and cheerfully to the policies already made or still to be made, provided such policies do not conflict with the Word of God.

Membership – Example #2

COMMUNICANT MEMBERSHIP

1. Definition

Communicant members are those baptized members who have been confirmed in the faith, accept the Doctrinal standards of Article III of this constitution, are familiar with at least the contents of the Catechism, who are not members of organizations whose principles and conduct conflict with the Word of God.

2. Reception

Communicant members are received through the rite of confirmation, by transfer from a sister congregation, upon profession of faith, or by reaffirmation of faith, providing that they conform to the requirements of membership in this congregation. Their reception shall be approved by the Board of Directors.

3. Duties

Communicant members shall conform their entire lives to the rule of God's Word and to that end make diligent use of the Means of Grace, exercise faithful stewardship of God's gifts, and impart and accept Christian admonition as the need for such becomes apparent.

Membership – Example #3

COMMUNICANT MEMBERSHIP

1. By confirmation: Persons received by confirmation in the congregation become communicant members.
2. By transfer or letter of reference: Persons coming with a communicant letter of transfer or coming with a letter of reference from another congregation of our denomination may be received by the Board of Directors.
3. By profession of faith: Other persons shall submit their application to a Pastor or to the Board of Directors, and having given satisfactory evidence of qualification, shall be received by the Board of Directors.

Terminating Membership – Example #4

II. TERMINATION OF MEMBERSHIP

A. Baptized membership shall be terminated for the following reasons:
   1. Members whose parent(s) receive a transfer (to a congregation in fellowship with us) or a letter of reference (to a congregation not in fellowship with us) or are released from membership, and for whose spiritual care we can, therefore, no longer share responsibility.
   2. Members whose parent(s) fail to have them instructed and/or confirmed (Article V, A, 4), providing they are capable of such instruction, by their sixteenth birthday.
B. Communicant membership shall be terminated for the following reasons:
   1. Members who request and receive transfers (to a congregation in fellowship with us) or a letter of reference (to a congregation not in fellowship with us). Such requests shall be acted upon by the Board of Directors and shall be reported to the Voters' Assembly.
   2. Members who move away and have not maintained contact for one year. Such action shall be reported to the Board of Directors, which in turn shall recommend that the Voters' Assembly declare their self-exclusion or termination of membership.
   3. Members who fail or refuse to submit to discipline, thereby excluding themselves.
   4. Members who, in spite of all admonition according to Matthew 18:15-20, refuse to amend, and are therefore excommunicated.
   5. Every resolution for self-exclusion or excommunication by the Voters' Assembly shall be unanimous. When such self-excluded or excommunicated person repents and seeks forgiveness from God and the congregation, he or she shall be reinstated.
C. Voting membership shall be terminated by termination of communicant membership.

Terminating Membership – Example #5

Termination

   a. Communicant members may be transferred to a sister congregation upon their request, by approval of the Senior Pastor or the Board of Directors.
   b. Communicant members who join congregations outside our fellowship thereby terminate their membership. Their names shall be removed from the membership.
   c. Communicant members whose whereabouts are unknown and whose addresses cannot be established.
   d. Communicant members who conduct themselves in a non-Christian manner shall be admonished according to Matthew 18:15-20: if they remain impenitent, they shall be excommunicated. A unanimous vote of the Board of Directors shall be required for excommunication.

Voting Membership – Example #1

C. <u>Voting Members</u>
   All confirmed members shall be voting members. It is expected of all voting members that they shall:
   1. Attend all meetings of the Voters' Assembly faithfully;
   2. Serve faithfully, according to their God-given talents, in any capacity in which they may be called upon to serve.

Voting Membership – Example #2

ARTICLE 2. VOTING MEMBERSHIP
Communicant members of this congregation who are 18 years of age or over, both male and female, shall be eligible to apply to become a Voting Member. Such application shall be made at any meeting of the Voters' Assembly. Upon affirmation of their intention to fulfill the responsibilities of membership to the best of their ability and that they have been provided a copy of the Constitution/Bylaws, applicants shall be received by the Voters' Assembly.

Voting Membership – Example #3

VOTING MEMBERSHIP
1. Definition
    Voting members are communicant members of the congregation who have reached the age of 16 years.
2. Duties
    Voting members shall attend the meeting of the congregation when such meetings are called.

Voters Meeting – Example #4

ARTICLE I: VOTERS' ASSEMBLY

A.   Meetings

The Voters' Assembly shall meet at least annually. The day and hour of the annual meeting shall be set by the Board of Directors and publicized at least two weeks in advance. The notification shall contain an agenda of items to be considered as well as the slate of nominees for election. The Voters' Assembly may meet at other times of the year subject to a call by the Board of Directors, or at the request of any twelve (12) voting members. Notice of any such special meeting shall be publicized as far in advance as possible but no less than one week in advance. The notice shall contain an agenda of items to be considered. No agenda items may be added once notification of any meeting is publicized. The Chairman, Vice Chairman, or their designated Board member shall preside at all Voters' Assembly meetings.

B.   Ouorum

A quorum of fifty (50) of the voting membership must be present to conduct the business of the Voters' Assembly.

Voters Meeting – Example #5

CONGREGATION MEETING

A.   Meeting

Meetings of the congregation shall be called by the Board of Directors by publicly announcing the date and place at least two Sundays prior to the date of the meeting. The congregation shall have the right to take up any items of business which are presented at these meetings.

B.   Quorum

Ordinarily the voters present at a properly called meeting shall constitute a quorum to do business. However, for amending the Constitution, or for the removal of a Pastor or other called person, a majority of all voting members shall be required for a quorum. In the absence of a majority, those present may fix the date for an adjourned meeting for which at least 5 days notice shall be given. The members who are present at such an adjourned meeting shall constitute a quorum.

Voters Meeting – Example #6

III. VOTERS' MEETINGS

A.   Regular meetings of the Voters' Assembly shall be held twice a year in the months of April and November.

Office of Called Worker – Example #1

ARTICLE VI: THE OFFICES OF PASTOR AND TEACHER

The pastoral office of this congregation as well as that of a called teacher in the Christian Day School shall be conferred upon only such ministers, teachers and candidates as profess and adhere to the confessional standards set forth in Article III of this constitution and who are well qualified for their work. Pastors and teachers shall, in the call extended to and accepted by them, be pledged to this confessional standard.

Office of Called Worker – Example #2

VII. OFFICES OF PASTOR, TEACHER, OTHER STAFF

A.   The office of Pastor in this congregation and that of called Teacher and other called staff shall be conferred only upon such Ministers, Teachers, and candidates who profess and adhere to the Confession of the Church (Article II) and who have been declared eligible by the Synod. Pastors and Teachers shall, in the call extended and accepted by them, be pledged to this confessional standard.

B.   Contract Teachers shall be hired by the School Board and shall be pledged to the Confessions of the Church (Article II).

C.   Approval to establish any new position shall be obtained from the congregation. After such approval, the hiring for the new (non-called) position shall be the responsibility of the board requesting such a position.

Calling a Called Worker – Example #3

PROCEDURE FOR SECURING A PASTOR, MINISTER OR TEACHER
1. The Call Committee
    a. The Board of Directors shall constitute the Call Committee for a pastor or minister, and the Standing Committee on Christian Day School for a principal or teacher.
    b. The Call Committee shall request a list of candidates and all available information concerning them from the District President or his representative.
    c. The list of candidates for pastor, principal, minister, or teacher shall be compiled by the Call Committee. The Committee should seek candidate names through soliciting the congregation membership, by contacting official sources in denominational offices, and through consultation with other appropriate sources related to the area of ministry for which a staff member is being sought. The Call Committee is to secure all pertinent information regarding each candidate in order that such information can be shared with the Voters' Assembly at the time of the call.
2. Election
    a. At a subsequent regular or special meeting of the Voters' Assembly one of the proposed candidates shall be elected by ballot and simple majority.
    b. It shall be the duty of the Chairman or Principal to see that notice of his or her election is delivered promptly to the candidate in whatever manner he shall deem advisable.
    c. Negotiations for a teacher assuming the duties of a position already established in the school staff may be delegated to the Standing Committee on Christian Day School. Such action is to be ratified by the Board of Directors.
    d. The establishing of a previously unheld or eliminated position on staff requires Voters' approval prior to a call or contract being issued.

Calling a Called Worker – Example #4

The pastoral office of this congregation as well as other called positions shall be conferred only on those who profess and adhere to the confessional standard set forth in Article III, Section B of this Constitution and who are qualified and rostered by the denomination for their work. Pastors and other called persons shall be pledged to this confessional standard.

A. Calling into Office
    1. After authorization is received from the Voters' Assembly, the Board of Directors shall create a Call Committee. At least halt of the Call Committee members shall not also be members of the Board of Directors.
    2. The Call Committee shall consult with those in the affected ministry area and with the district office as part of their efforts to secure the names of candidates.
    3. The Call Committee will present a final list of candidates to the Voters' Assembly for issuance of the call.

Removal of a Called Worker – Example #5

REMOVAL FROM OFFICE
Any pastor, or other called worker, officer or board member, who fails to perform the duties of confirmed members as stated in Article V, or is unable or is willfully neglectful in the performance of his official duties, may be removed from office in Christian love and lawful order by the Voters' Assembly. Such action shall be initiated through a member of the Board of Directors.

Removal of a Called Worker – Example #6

B. Removal from Office
Any pastor or other called person may be removed from office by the Voters by a two-thirds majority secret ballot vote for one of the following reasons: Persistent adherence to false doctrine, scandalous life, or neglect of duties.

Removal of a Called Worker – Example #7

DISCIPLINE
Section 1. Provisions Pertaining to Church Officers and Board of Directors
Any person holding an elected position of the congregation who neglects the duties of such office may be removed from office by a three-fifths (3/5) majority vote of the Voting Members present in a meeting of the Voters' Assembly. The Board of Directors shall initiate such disciplinary action.
Section 2. Provisions Pertaining to the Pastors and Other Called Servants
In Christian love and lawful order, any called worker may be removed from office by the Voters' Assembly for any of the following reasons: persistent adherence to false doctrine, scandalous life, willful neglect or inability to perform the duties of office as included in the Bylaws (Article 5) and the applicable Call document.

The Board of Directors shall carefully investigate charges on any of these counts. Should such charges be substantiated by clear evidence, and after consultation with the District President or his designated representative, the Board of Directors shall notify the Voting Members of the situation and submit the matter for action at a special meeting of that body. Such meeting shall be announced by mail at least two weeks in advance of the meeting and at regular worship services on the preceding two weekends. All Voting Members shall be notified of such meeting by mail at least two weeks in advance.

A three-fifths (3/5) vote of the Voting Members present at Voters' Assembly shall be required to remove any divinely called servant from office.

Officers - Example #1
ARTICLE III: DUTIES OF OFFICERS
A. Chairman - The duties of the Chairman shall be as follows:
1. Preside at all meetings of the Voters' Assembly and the Board of Directors.
2. Appoint any necessary committees.
3. Sign all legal documents, with the Secretary, on behalf of the congregation.
4. Enforce the constitution and bylaws and perform the general duties as are common for the office, including such additional duties as may be directed by the Voters' Assembly from time to time.
B. Vice-Chairman - The duties of the Vice-Chairman shall be as follows:
1. Perform all of the duties of the Chairman in the latter's absence and such other additional duties which may be directed by the Voters' Assembly or by the Chairman from time to time.
2. Chair and appoint a Nominating Committee with the advice and consent of the Board of Directors.
C. Secretary - The duties of the Secretary shall be as follows:
1. The duties shall be those commonly required of that office, especially the keeping and preserving of accurate records of all Voters' Assembly meetings, and handling such correspondence as the congregation may require.
2. Sign all legal documents, with the Chairman, on behalf of the congregation.
3. Keep minutes of all Board of Directors meetings.
D. Treasurer - The duties of the Treasurer shall be as follows:
1. Keep and preserve the accurate records of all receipts and disbursements, and submit a written report of them at all regular meetings of the Voters' Assembly.
2. Pay all regular and fixed expenses on order of the Voters' Assembly.

Officers - Example #2

Article II, OFFICERS

The Officers of the Congregation shall consist of a Chairman, Vice-Chairman Secretary and Treasurer. Any voting member may hold these offices, except that the office of Chairman and Vice-Chairman may be occupied by males only.

Officers - Example #3
ARTICLE 7: DUTIES OF THE OFFICES
Section 1. President
The President shall:
a. Preside at all meetings of the Voters' Assembly and shall call and preside over meetings of the Board of Directors.
b. To the best of his ability, enforce the Constitution and Bylaws of the congregation and carry out the expressed will of the congregation as embodied in the resolutions of the Voting Membership and sign all legal documents on behalf of the congregation.
c. With the approval of the Board of Directors, appoint members of Policy Advisory and Ad Hoc committees as established by the Voters' Assembly or the Board of Directors.
d. At the direction of the Board of Directors, call special meetings of the Voters' Assembly. Be a non-voting member of all Boards, committees, auxiliaries, groups, etc., in the congregation and shall be welcome at all their meetings either in person or represented by such person(s) he may appoint
Section 2. Vice President
The Vice President shall act for and in the stead of the President in his/her absence and shall be available for whatever duties the President may assign.
Section 3. Secretary/Treasury
The Secretary/Treasurer shall:
a. Sign legal documents on behalf of the congregation where more than one signature is required;
b. Assure prompt payment of all expenditures authorized by the Voters' Assembly or the Board of Directors, and coordination of such payments to maintain the financial integrity of the congregation;
c. Assure accurate record keeping of all congregational receipts and disbursements;
d. Furnish periodic financial reports to the Voters' Assembly and Board of Directors;
e. Be a non-voting member of the Advisory Committee on Finance.

Election of Officers – Example #4

ARTICLE 2: OFFICERS

1. <u>Nominating Committee</u> - The Vice Chairman of the Board shall annually appoint a Nominating Committee whose responsibility will be to develop a slate of officers and Board members to be elected each year to fill the vacancies created by expired terms of officers and board members. The committee shall contain a majority of non-board members, shall function for one year only, and shall report their nominations to the Voters' Assembly annual meeting. The Senior Pastor shall be a non-voting member of the Nominating Committee. All nominees shall be voting members.

2. <u>Elections and Terms of Office</u> - The members of the Board of Directors shall be elected by the Voters' Assembly. The term of office shall be for a maximum of two years, with approximately one half of the Board being elected each year. Board members shall serve no more than two full successive terms. Immediately following the election of the new Board members, the Voters' Assembly shall elect a Chairman, Vice Chairman, Secretary and Treasurer from the members of the Board. These officers shall be elected for a one-year term. Every term of office shall begin on January I following the election. In the event of a vacancy on the Board of Directors, the Nominating Committee shall provide the Chairman with a list of candidates. Appointments to fill unexpired terms will be made from such list and must be ratified by a majority vote of the Board. The individual shall serve until the next election for that particular position. In addition to the Nominating Committee's slate of candidates, any voting member may nominate any other Board positions. Such nominations shall be called for in the annual Voters' Assembly meeting prior to the time that nominations are closed.

Election of Officers – Example #5

Article IV, NOMINATION AND ELECTION OF OFFICERS

1. Nomination Procedure

   The Chairman of the Congregation will select a Nominating Committee of not less than four (4) voting members including the Senior Pastor. The Nominating Committee will prepare a single slate of candidates drawn from communicant members, 18 years of age or older. The Nominating Committee will check with each candidate as to their willingness to serve before placing their names in nomination. The following officers shall be nominated: Chairman, Vice-Chairman, Secretary and Treasurer. The Nominating Committee, at least two weeks before the date of the election, shall publish a list of the candidates in the Church Bulletin or newsletter.

2. Election Procedure

   At the annual meeting of the Voters' Assembly the officers shall be elected by a simple majority of voters present and voting.

3. Vacancies of Elected Offices

   In the event that the position of Chairman or any other officer is vacated, the Church Council will appoint a person to fill that position for the remainder of the unexpired term.

4. Term of Office

   The term of office of all Officers shall be two (2) years. They shall assume their duties immediately following their election. The Chairman of the Congregation or other Church Officer who has served two full terms shall not succeed themselves in office, except by approval of a two-thirds majority vote of the eligible voters present at a scheduled Voters' Assembly.

Lay Leadership Group – Example #1

THE BOARD OF DIRECTORS
A. Duties
The Board of Directors, as the chief governing board of the congregation, shall act in all matters pertaining to the general welfare of file congregation, except the calling of a Pastor or staff person, the purchase or sale of land or buildings (other than staff housing), or entering into a building program requiring the borrowing of funds. The Board of Directors shall also review the activities and reports of the Board of Elders and the Board of Property and Finance and the staff. The Board of Directors shall concern itself with making all policy governing the activities of file church. It shall oversee and provide for the professional staff of the church. It shall concern itself with the theology and mission of the church as outlined in Articles II and III of the Constitution, seeing to it that all activities of the church reflect the theology and mission of the church and the Gospel of Jesus Christ. It shall concern itself with planning and vision for the future. It shall have authority over all other Boards and committees of the congregation. The Board of Directors may appoint such task forces or committees as needed.
B. Membership
The Board of Directors shall consist of nine members and the Chairperson of the Boards of Elders and Property/Finance. The Board of Directors shall annually elect its own Chairperson, Vice-chairperson and Secretary who then shall also serve as the Chairperson, Vice-chairperson and Secretary of the congregation.
C. Meetings
The Board of Directors shall ordinarily meet in regular session monthly. The Senior Pastor, the Chairperson, or any three members of the Board of Directors may call special meetings by personally informing each member of tile Board of Directors of tile time and place of such meeting. A majority of voting members of tile Board of Directors shall constitute a quorum.

Lay Leadership Group – Example #2

ARTICLE III, THE BOARD OF DIRECTORS
1. Membership
The Board of Directors shall consist of at least eight members made up of the Church officers, a representative from the Elders, the Senior Pastor and members at large. The Chairman of the Congregation shall be the Chairman of the Board of Directors. The Congregational Secretary shall serve as recording secretary.
2. Duties
It shall be the duty of the Board of Directors to consider and discuss all matters pertaining to the general welfare of the Congregation, to establish a call procedure and to present recommendations to the Voters' Assembly. The Board of Directors shall have the responsibility and authority to decide on all matters not specifically reserved for Voters' Assembly decision. The Council will have the responsibility to designate those who have the authority to sign official Church documents and contracts.
3. Meetings
The Board of Directors shall meet at least quarterly at a time and place determined by the Congregational Chairman. The Senior Pastor or Chairman of the Congregation may call special meetings of the Council by informing members of the time and place of such meetings at least twenty-four (24) hours in advance.
4. Quorum and Decisions
A majority of members present shall constitute a quorum. Decisions of the Council will be made by a simple majority of those members voting. The presiding Chairman shall not vote except in case of ties.
5. Committees
The Congregational Chairman, in consultation with the Senior Pastor, has the responsibility of recommending the establishment of or the dissolution of Committees. They also have the responsibility of recommending the Chairperson and others who shall chair such Committees. Their recommendations shall be referred to the Board of Directors for decision. The Congregational Chairman shall furnish to each Committee Chairperson a job description for their respective Committee.

Lay Leadership Group – Example #3

ARTICLE 8. FUNCTIONS POWERS AND ORGANIZATI0N OF THE BOARD OF DIRECTOR AND MINISTRY STAFF

Section 1 - Board of Directors

The Board of Directors shall be comprised of the officers, nine (9) other voting members elected by the congregation (or appointed to fill vacancies as provided in the Bylaws) and the Executive Pastor. As empowered by the Constitution (Article 4) and Bylaws (Article 4, Section 1) the Board of Directors shall conduct and perform the acts and affairs of the congregation in its stead between Annual meetings of the Voters' Assembly.

Under the Chairman and with the guidance of the Pastor(s), the Board of Directors shall:
A. Be responsible for establishing policies necessary to direct the overall program of the congregation for the furtherance of Christ's Kingdom in our midst;
B. Maintain the financial integrity of the congregation;
C. Encourage the Ministry Staff in their work through prayer, word and action and provide for the spiritual and physical health and welfare of the Ministry Staff and their families;
D. Exercise with the Pastor(s) discipline within the congregation with respect to all matters of membership of the congregation as provided in the Constitution and Bylaws;
E. Authorize the Ministry Staff to administer the day-to-day operations of the congregation in accordance with its own policies and directives and those established by the congregation through its Voters' Assembly;
F. Direct the calling of special meetings of the Voters' Assembly as requested by the Pastor(s) or voting members;
G. Be responsible for the receiving of and acting upon, if necessary, feed-back and/or complaints from members of the congregation regarding aspects of its operations;
H. Establish appropriate Policy Advisory and Ad hoc (i.e., Nominating, Auditing, W, etc.) committees and approve the appointment of members;
I. Appoint persons to fill unexpired terms of members of Board of Directors;
J. Be available for any additional functions that the Voters' Assembly may confer on it.

The Board of Directors will be responsible for maintenance of a manual of congregational policies to assist in the uniform and consistent administration of affairs of the congregation. The manual shall not include any provision contrary to this Constitution and Bylaws concerning membership in the congregation; the rights and duties of persons holding office, Board of Directors and pastors or other called servants. It shall not create any contract rights not otherwise authorized in a manner set forth by this Constitution and Bylaws. Only the Voters' Assembly shall have the power to modify the manual with respect to sections dealing with functions of Pastor, officers, and Board of Directors.

The Board of Directors shall meet monthly. Additional meetings may be called by the President or the Pastor(s) as required.

Section 2. Ministry Staff

The Board of Directors' responsibility is generally confined to establishing topmost policies, leaving implementation and subsidiary policy development to the Executive Pastor. All board authority delegated to staff is delegated through the Executive Pastor. The Executive Pastor is to provide regular reports to the Board of Directors on the status of all operations. As authorized by the Board of Directors, the Ministry Staff shall conduct the day-to-day business of the congregation.

Appendix D
Notes to Subgroups

Membership subgroup   Page 75

Voters subgroup   Page 76

Called Workers subgroup   Page 77

Officers   Page 78

Lay Leadership Group   Page 79

Subgroup tasks	Subgroup method
1. Read the list of major questions 2. Read the draft wording 3. Read the current wording 4. Answer the major questions (avoid wordsmithing) 5. Select someone to orally report major concepts to the full group	1. Discuss questions in teams of two 2. Share major thoughts 3. Take "straw polls" 4. Made preliminary decision or Capture major options for full group discussion

Notes for Membership – Draft Bylaws Articles 1 and 2

• See the current constitution/bylaws, page ___, Article ___, Section ___.

1. Shall we include statements of doctrinal standards (Example #1, Sections A and B; and Example #2)?

2. Shall we list the methods by which a person can become a communicant member (Example #3)?

3. Who can receive a person into communicant membership by profession of faith (Example #2, Section 2 and Example #3, Section 3)?
   – The senior pastor
   – Any other pastor
   – the Lay Leadership Group or their designee

The classification of Voting Membership is being handled by the group dealing with the Voters' Assembly subgroup.

Notes for Terminating Membership – Draft Bylaws Article 4

• See the current constitution/bylaws, page ___, Article ___, Section ___.

1. Shall we be as detailed as in Example #4, or more compact as in Example #5?

2. Will we permit excommunication? If so, who makes that determination?
   – The Voters (requiring public airing of the issues)?
   – The Senior Pastor?
   – Any other pastors?
   – The Lay Leadership Group or their designee?

Caution: Historically, many congregations used the term "excommunication" when they actually meant "removal from congregation membership." Excommunication has a theological connotation of "separation from God and the hope of salvation." In current times, large numbers of congregations have decided that matters between God and individuals should be left to God. These congregations chose simply to exercise their authority of "removal from congregation membership."

Subgroup tasks	**Subgroup method**
1. Read the list of major questions 2. Read the draft wording 3. Read the current wording 4. Answer the major questions (avoid wordsmithing) 5. Select someone to orally report major concepts to the full group	1. Discuss questions in teams of two 2. Share major thoughts 3. Take "straw polls" 4. Made preliminary decision or Capture major options for full group discussion

Notes for Voting Membership – Draft Bylaws Article 3

* See the current constitution/bylaws, page ___, Article ___, Section ___.

1. What is the minimum age to vote at voters meetings (all three examples)?
   A growing number of congregations are allowing voting after confirmation. The young members greatly appreciate the gesture. Some people feel this is not appropriate because younger members "cannot understand the issues." Others point out that many adults do not "understand the issues." In our consulting practice we always receive some of the most accurate understanding of what is truly happening in congregations from the teenagers we interview.

2. Shall a list of duties be prescribed (Examples #1 and #3)?
   The lists of duties in the examples look nice, but can be a source of discord in a dispute. For example, what does "attend all meetings … faithfully" mean? If you miss one are you out? Also, what does "serve" mean, and if you do not "serve" are you no longer a voter?

3. Shall Voting Membership be automatic (Example #1 and #3) or require action of the Voters' Assembly (Example #2)?

Notes for Voters' Assembly – Draft Bylaws Article 5

* See the current constitution/bylaws, page ___, Article ___, Section ___.

1. Shall a Voters' Assembly be required at least once a year (Example #4, Section A) or twice a year (Example #6, Section A)?
   Meeting more than twice a year probably means the voters are dealing with too many operational details.

2. Who can call for a Special Voters' Meeting?
   – the congregation Chair?
   – the Lay Leadership Group?
   – the Senior Pastor?
   – a fixed number of voters (Example #4, Section A)? If so, how many voters need to sign the petition calling for the meeting?

3. Shall the advance notice for a Special Voters' Meeting be two weeks (all three examples) or some other number of weeks?

4. Shall a quorum constitute all those in attendance (Example #5, Section B) or a specific number of members (Example #4, Section B)?

Subgroup tasks	**Subgroup method**
1. Read the list of major questions 2. Read the draft wording 3. Read the current wording 4. Answer the major questions (avoid wordsmithing) 5. Select someone to orally report major concepts to the full group	1. Discuss questions in teams of two 2. Share major thoughts 3. Take "straw polls" 4. Made preliminary decision or Capture major options for full group discussion

Notes for Called Workers – Draft Bylaws Article 6

- See the current constitution/bylaws, page ___, Article ___, Section ___.

1. For churches with a parochial school, shall teachers be limited to those on the official roster of the denomination (Example #2, Section A)?

2. (Note: Contract teachers who are not issued a "divine call" are not covered in the bylaws.)

Notes for Calling a Called Worker – Draft Bylaws Article 6

- See the current constitution/bylaws, page ___, Article ___, Section ___.

1. Shall the Call Committee be an existing group (Lay Leadership Group for pastor or minister, and School Board for principal or teacher) as in Example #3, or a group assembled for that purpose as in Example #4?

2. If the Call Committee is a group assembled for that purpose, who shall appoint the Call Committee?

Notes for Removal of Called Worker – Draft Bylaws Article 6

- See the current constitution/bylaws, page ___, Article ___, Section ___.

Note: In current times, while it is helpful to list only a few examples of reasons for removal, the language should be clear that these are examples and not a comprehensive list. It is impossible to predict all possible reasons for removal. In the end, reasons for removal from office actually comes down to any activity to which the congregation's Voters' Assembly objects.

1. Shall the Voters of the congregation have the right to remove a called worker from office?

2. Shall the Voters' Assembly vote for removal be simple majority (50% in Example #5), three-fifths (60% in Example 7, last paragraph), two-thirds (67% is the standard for changing the Constitution), or some other percentage?

Subgroup tasks	**Subgroup method**
1. Read the list of major questions 2. Read the draft wording 3. Read the current wording 4. Answer the major questions (avoid wordsmithing) 5. Select someone to orally report major concepts to the full group	1. Discuss questions in teams of two 2. Share major thoughts 3. Take "straw polls" 4. Made preliminary decision <div align="center">or</div>Capture major options for full group discussion

Notes for Officers – Draft Bylaws Article 7, Sections A – D

- See the current constitution/bylaws, page ___, Article ___, Section ___.

Decisions

1. Shall we use the term President, Chairman, Chairperson, or something else?

2. Shall the Vice Chair, the Chair, or the Lay Leadership Group appoint the nominating committee (Example 1, Section B2 and Example 2, Section A)?

3. Shall the Chair and Vice Chair be limited to males only (Example 2)?

4. Shall we have a combination Secretary/Treasurer, or two positions (Example 3, Section 3)? This is possible in very small congregations. It is possible in large congregations where the Treasurer has no check writing responsibility.

5. What will be the length of the term of office?

6. When shall the term of office begin?

Notes for Election of Officers and Lay Leadership Group – Draft Bylaws Article 11

- See the current constitution/bylaws, page ___, Article ___, Section ___.

Decisions

7. Shall the Senior Pastor be a non-voting member of the Nominating Committee (Example 4, Section 1) or a voting member (Example 5, Section 1)?

8. Shall there by a requirement of nominating more than one person to each available position (not in either example)?

9. Shall the Senior Leadership Board or some other group be authorized to appoint a person to fill an unexpired term (Example 2, Section 3)?

Subgroup tasks	Subgroup method
1. Read the list of major questions	1. Discuss questions in teams of two
2. Read the draft wording	2. Share major thoughts
3. Read the current wording	3. Take "straw polls"
4. Answer the major questions (avoid wordsmithing)	4. Made preliminary decision
5. Select someone to orally report major concepts to the full group	or
	Capture major options for full group discussion

Notes for Lay Leadership Group – Draft Bylaws Articles 8, 9, and 10

- See the current constitution/bylaws, page ___, Article ___, Section ___.

1. What will be the name of this group? Some examples are:
   a. Board of Directors
   b. Mission and Ministry Council
   c. Ministry Council
   d. Mission Council
   e. Vestry
   f. Session

2. In addition to the congregation officers, how many will be voting members? Most congregations using this format have a total of no fewer than seven nor more than eleven.

   Some traditions call for a group of twenty-five or more people. This is entirely too many people. It is many more than is needed to have an effective group. More importantly, it consumes far too many volunteer resources that are often needed in other ministries. Careful consideration should be given before continuing this tradition left over from the churched culture.

3. What will be the length of the term of office?

4. Shall the Senior Pastor be a voting member or a non-voting member?

5. Shall they be required to meet a minimum of once a month (Example #1, Section C), or quarterly (Example #2, Section 3)?
   Requiring quarterly meetings represents a minimum frequency. The group is free to meet more often.

6. Shall we list the primary responsibilities of this group (Example 3, Section 1, Points A – J)?

7. Shall we specifically state that the group sets policies and the Senior Pastor implements policies (Example #3, Section 2)

8. How many Lay Leadership Group members shall constitute a quorum?

Election process for the Lay Leadership Group is included in the group discussing election of the officers.

Appendix E
Draft Policy Manuals

Lay Leadership Group   Page 81

Boards, Committees, Teams,   Page 85
    and Other Groups

Policy Manual
Lay Leadership Group
First Church

A. DESIRED OUTCOMES POLICY

As led by the Holy Spirit, it is the desired outcome of First Church that the Gospel of Jesus Christ is taught and lived in an environment of a growing and caring community in Christ. Through worship, word and sacrament ministry, discipleship, and Christian care, believers and non-believers are reached and nurtured in Christ and in a loving and accepting fellowship with each other.

The central mission of First Church is to:

Connect People with God and Others

Primary Ministry Outcomes:

	Last Year	This Year	Next Year	Third Year
1. Persons served in mission:	___	___	___	___
2. Constituents:	___	___	___	___
3. Average weekly worship attendance:	___	___	___	___
4. People Involvement Ratio: (People in ministries / average worship attendance)	___	___	___	___
5. Other numerical or narrative outcomes:	___	___	___	___

Secondary Ministry Outcomes:

	Last Year	This Year	Next Year	Third Year
6. Number of members:	___	___	___	___
7. Adult Bible class attendance:	___	___	___	___
8. Children's Sunday School attendance:	___	___	___	___
9. Other numerical or narrative outcomes:	___	___	___	___

B. LAY LEADERSHIP GROUP
SELF-GOVERNANCE POLICIES

Introduction

1. The principal function shall be to develop, monitor, and enforce policy, not to implement it.

2. Except for assignments of work to its own subcommittees, the Group shall delegate authority only to the Senior Pastor. Other staff or entities shall receive their authority from the Senior Pastor or person acting on behalf of the Senior Pastor.

3. The Group shall address only broad areas, leaving lesser levels to the Senior Pastor whose authority begins where explicit pronouncements of the Group end. Except where required by policy or law, decisions of the Senior Pastor do not need approval from the Lay Leadership Group.

Member Policies

1. Members shall actively participate in the worship, Christian growth, and educational activities of First Church.

2. Members shall seek to develop their own personal spiritual life through the use of devotions, prayer, Bible study, and the practice of Christian stewardship.

3. Members shall seek to grow as Christian leaders by continually striving to increase their understanding of the theology, mission, and ministry of First Church.

4. Members shall attend and participate in all scheduled meetings, not missing more than two consecutive meetings without a valid excuse reported to the chair.

5. Members shall relate to each other as members of the Body of Christ with openness, integrity, honesty, and Christian love.

6. Members shall be open to opinions and concerns that may be expressed to them by members of the congregation. All such information shall remain confidential with the member except as they may share this information with the chair and the Lay Leadership Group as a whole when deemed appropriate.

7. Members who violate any of these policies shall be subject to review and action by the Group as a whole.

Meeting Policies

1. Meetings shall be conducted under the guidelines of Robert's Rules of Order. The chair shall be responsible for the preparation of the agenda and determining of the content of the meeting. Members may insert items onto the agenda with agreement of a majority of those attending that meeting.

2. The meeting agenda of the shall include:
   a. Opportunity for growth in the theology and mission of the church
   b. The Senior Pastor's report
   c. Policy and governance issues
   d. Periodic reports from boards, committees, task forces, action teams, and organizations affiliated with the congregation
   e. Opening and closing prayer

3. They shall maintain policies in the areas of Desired Outcomes Policies, Lay Leadership Group Self Governance Policies, Lay Leadership Group and Senior Pastor Relations Policies, and Senior Pastor Policies.

4. Policies are to be active and dynamic. They are to be reviewed, changed, and refined. There shall be an annual review of all policies with emphasis on how a policy affects the ministry and mission of First Church.

5. The Group members shall keep documents and discussions confidential unless permission to act otherwise is granted by the chair or majority vote by the Group.

6. The Group shall annually review itself focusing on communication, faithfulness to the theology of the church, the mission and ministry of First Church, and adherence to its own policies.

7. The Group shall keep the congregation informed of its activities and actively seek feedback from the membership of the church.

C. LAY LEADERSHIP GROUP AND SENIOR PASTOR RELATIONS

1. The function of the Lay Leadership Group shall be to develop, monitor, and enforce policy, not to implement it.

2. Except for assignments of work to its own subcommittees and others, it shall delegate authority only to the Senior Pastor. Other staff or entities shall receive their authority from the Senior Pastor or person acting on his behalf.

3. The Group shall address only broad areas, leaving lesser levels to the Senior Pastor whose authority begins where explicit pronouncements of the Group end. Except where required by policy or law, decisions of the Senior Pastor do not need approval from the Group.

4. The Senior Pastor shall be accountable to the Group for:
   a. Accomplishing the mission and ministry of First Church.
   b. Conducting all ministry in keeping with the standards of faith and practice of First Church.
   c. Ensuring compliance of all staff with the policies of First Church.
   d. Providing the Group adequate information to carry out its tasks.
   e. Relating with integrity, honesty, and straightforwardness to the Group.
   f. Reporting to the Group on any incident that may be deemed to impact the congregational or worship life of First Church.

5. The Group shall monitor the following:
   a. Regular reports from the Senior Pastor on primary and secondary ministry outcomes.
   b. Personnel policies and staff job descriptions.
   c. Long term vision and outlook.
   d. Other significant matters determined by the Lay Leadership Group or Senior Pastor.

D. SENIOR PASTOR
LIMITATIONS POLICY

1. As representatives of First Church, neither the Senior Pastor nor any staff member shall act in a manner that may be judged unethical, illegal, or inconsistent with the constitution, bylaws, articles of incorporation, or Group policies of First Church.

2. The Senior Pastor shall not allow First Church to operate in a financial manner that may jeopardize the mission of First Church. The Senior Pastor shall not allow financial management to operate outside the generally accepted principles of accounting procedure, and not allow any expenditure that is not sufficiently funded.

3. The Senior Pastor shall not allow positions to be undefined and not allow position descriptions to exist that may inaccurately describe the duties and responsibilities of a position.

4. The Senior Pastor shall not leave conflicts unresolved, but shall seek to resolve all conflicts quickly and in a Christian manner, being open to the views of all parties involved, so that the ministry and mission of First Church are not adversely affected.

5. The Senior Pastor shall not allow any communications that do not reflect the ministry and mission of First Church.

6. The Senior Pastor shall not permit any group to use First Church's facilities whose activities might conflict with the Desired Outcomes and faith of First Church without securing the approval of the Lay Leadership Group.

Education Ministry of First Church (Model for all Boards, Committees, Teams, and Other Groups)

A. DESIRED OUTCOMES

The Education Ministry is part of the overall ministry of First Church's efforts to:

Connect People With God and Others

To that end, the Education Ministry carries out a series of activities. However, the purpose of the activities is not simply to complete the activities. The purpose is to achieve primary and secondary ministry outcomes that contribute to achievement the whole congregation's ministry outcomes.

Primary ministry outcomes of the Education Ministry:

	Last Year	This Year	Next Year	Third Year
1. Persons served in mission by the Education Dept.:	_____	_____	_____	_____
2. Constituents:	_____	_____	_____	_____
3. People in ministries (numerator of Involvement Ratio):	_____	_____	_____	_____
4. Other numerical or narrative outcomes:	_____	_____	_____	_____

Secondary ministry outcomes of the Education Ministry:

	Last Year	This Year	Next Year	Third Year
5. Member adult Bible class attendance:	_____	_____	_____	_____
6. Member child Bible class attendance:	_____	_____	_____	_____
7. Levels of Biblical literacy in the congregation:	_____	_____	_____	_____
8. Other numerical or narrative outcomes:	_____	_____	_____	_____

B. PRIMARY ACTIVITIES

Children's Christian Education

1. Conduct weekly Sunday school for children.

2. Confirmation instruction for seventh and eighth graders.

3. Seventh and eighth grade Confirmation retreat as part of the Confirmation curriculum.

Adult Christian Education

1. Weekly Bible study classes for adults on Sunday.

2. Small group Bible study at other times weekly.

C. EDUCATION MINISTRY BOARD POLICIES

Duties

1. Create, adopt, and periodically review this Policy Manual.

2. Submit this Policy Manual to the congregation's Lay Leadership Group annually at a time agreed to with the Lay Leadership Group. Reach agreement with the Lay Leadership Group on the Desired Outcomes Policies of this manual.

3. Provide policy level guidance to the paid/volunteer staff in the operation of education programs and activities of the congregation.

Membership

1. The Education Ministry Board consists of seven members. At least four of the members must also be members of the congregation.

2. Each member serves a three-year term with no limit on the number of times an individual can be elected.

3. In spring of each year, the existing Board will nominate twice as many people to the Education Ministry Board as needed to fill open positions. Election to the Board is conducted at an event selected or created by the Board and open to all voting members of the congregation, participants in the activities who are age 18 or older, and parents of children participating in the activities.

Officers and Meetings

1. The members of the Education Ministry Board will select a Chair and Vice-Chair. The Chair is responsible for creating and distributing agendas, coordination with the paid/volunteer staff, and coordination with the congregation's Lay Leadership Group.

2. The Education Ministry Board will meet at least quarterly.

D. BOARD AND STAFF RELATIONS

1. The function of the Board shall be to develop, monitor, and enforce policy, not to implement it.

2. The Board shall address only broad areas, leaving lesser levels to the paid/volunteer staff whose authority begins where explicit pronouncements of the Board end.

3. The paid/volunteer staff shall be accountable to the Board for:
   a. Accomplishing the primary and secondary ministry outcomes of the Education Board.
   b. Conducting Education ministry in keeping with the faith standards and practices of First Church.
   c. Ensuring compliance of all paid/volunteer staff with the policies of the Education Board and applicable policies of the congregation.
   d. Providing the Board with adequate information to carry out its tasks.
   e. Relating with integrity, honesty, and straightforwardness to Board.
   f. Reporting to the Board on any incident that may be deemed to impact the congregation or Education Ministry.

4. The Board shall monitor the following:
   a. Regular reports from the paid/volunteer staff on activities and ministries.
   b. Regular financial reports expenses, receipts, status of the budget.
   c. Staff job descriptions.
   d. Regular reports on participation counts and progress to reaching outcome policies.

Appendix F
Notes for Event Facilitator

Congratulations on being willing to lead an exciting event that will make a meaningful difference in the life of the congregation. We invite you to look forward to inviting the Holy Spirit to assist in the event and then observe the effects that result from trusting in the Lord and in the missional spirit of members.

Appendix F is a series of specific suggestions based upon our experience in helping churches rewrite their constitution and bylaws in a one-day event. Completing a redraft in one day may seem to be a difficult or impossible undertaking. It is not—as long as the assembly is able to keep focused on the major decisions.

The following suggestions are listed approximately in the order they will be encountered:

1. Quickly read through the entire book to get the general idea of what is happening.

2. Some churches do not have a constitution. They will have bylaws containing most of the same content. Indeed, having only one document, the bylaws, is a more efficient way to operate.

   In that situation, you and the steering committee will want to modify Chapter 6, the draft in Appendix B, and the text of the presentations. A quick way to make the changes is to use the Microsoft® Word "Replace" command under the "Edit" menu. Simply replace "constitution and bylaws" with the word "bylaws." You will want to repeat that process to search for and remove the term "constitution." Each section of text can then easily be modified.

3. Help the congregation's leaders and the steering team understand that creating a new constitution is not the only issue being addressed. The more important matter is creating a new structure in such a way that the vast majority of the congregation embraces it with enthusiasm. Enthused and eager anticipation of a more effective way to be the church on earth also breathes renewed life into the congregation.

   It may be necessary to help the church's leaders and the steering team understand that the common method of appointing a relatively small "Constitution Committee" to complete the rewrite and then asking the Voters to approve the draft is an invitation to either of two disasters. One disaster can be strong resistance to final approval of the changed constitution and bylaws. The second is the possibility that the new document will be approved by a small group and then later rejected by the majority.

4. The first overall principle for drafting the document is to have the congregation make basic decisions about structure and procedures. Then you or one other person can turn those decisions into the appropriate language. Be careful to help the assembly and subgroups avoid becoming bogged down in specific wording or phrasing.

5. The second overall principle is to keep the process moving without the assembly feeling railroaded or stampeded. The best way to accomplish this is to stick to the procedures and questions listed in this

book. Sometimes the group needs to be reminded to make major decisions rather than dealing with specific wording.

6. The final overall principle is a reminder that strong opinions by a few people will often mask the opinion of the majority. Chapter 8 provides an explanation that is worth repeating here.

We frequently use a straw poll to assess the true feelings of the assembly without calling for a formal vote. A straw poll is an informal show of hands. Most people, including the strong-willed people dominating the discussion, will be comfortable with this approach.

The best way to describe usage and impact of this approach is with an example.

The members were discussing whether the congregation chairperson could be female. The current constitution prohibited women in that office. The denomination had disseminated mixed messages.

The assembly heard three people make statements on each side of the question. One side was that the idea was against biblical teachings, the denomination opposed it, and timing was not right. The other side contended that the Bible described women who had asserted spiritual leadership, the denomination only objected to women doing things that almost never come up, and most women are tired of and angry about being kept out of this office. The pastor responded to a question about this issue by stating that he could use biblical, historical, and denominational citations to support both positions.

The room seemed evenly divided and headed for an impasse. The statement that seemed to be carrying considerable weight was that "because so many changes were being instituted, we should delay this one."

We suggested that a straw poll be taken. We outlined all points of view on one side of the issue and then on the other. We called for a show of hands in favor of women being eligible for the chairperson

role. About eighty people raised their hands. We then asked for those opposed. Only five people held up their hands, the three speakers and two others. This matter that seemed about to stop the event proved to be a non-issue.

In addition to keeping the group going, the straw poll achieved two helpful outcomes. First, it showed that the group was firmly on one side of the issue, ending the discussion by showing the other side they were the clear minority.

The second outcome is critical. Many congregations have a very small group who will literally hold the majority hostage to their own point of view. Because they only discuss their perspective with a few friends, they have the impression that their viewpoint reflects a large portion of the church. The straw poll approach is an effective way of releasing the majority from the tyranny of a few strong-willed people.

7. Denominations sometimes intervene in local church decisions. Some denominations have the practice of approving, or not approving, the church's constitution and by-laws.

We use a general rule of thumb that the congregation should make the decision they feel is best for their ministry. The denomination can make its own decision about the church's choice. Normally, discussion with the denomination's group that reviews these documents will lead to an acceptable wording. Do not let the meeting become bogged down in guessing about what the denomination might or might not approve.

8. Help the event steering team grasp the importance of adhering to the many suggestions provided in Chapter 5. If changes have to be made, help them realistically understand the likely impact of those changes.

9. Help the steering team understand the value of providing all of the printed support materials in sufficient quantities that everyone has a copy. Sharing copies slows down the process, especially when the subgroups are discussing the alternate wordings of bylaws (Appendix C). Having their own copy gives the participants comfort that they are giving their subgroup issues due consideration.

10. Sometimes it is necessary to help the steering team understand that under no circumstances should the draft provided in Appendix B be distributed to the event participants. No amount of explanation will overcome the feeling held by many that the new constitution and bylaws have already been written, and that this event is just to rubber-stamp what someone else has already done.

11. You, and perhaps someone from the congregation, will want to go through the key questions listed in Chapter 6. Remove those that do not apply, and add any that are needed. Be sure to add only those that are major issues. Do not add relatively minor matters or issues that will be considered by the subgroups.

    As you consider the new constitution, carefully read any clauses in the existing constitution that are "unalterable." It is best not to make any changes in the intent of these provisions. When that happens, only one disgruntled person can stop the whole process by appealing to the denomination or local legal system. Improving, clarifying, or simplifying language is less of a potential problem.

12. Review the subgroups called for in Chapter 7. Remove those that do not apply, and add any that represent major additions not covered in the draft constitution and bylaws (Appendix B) or subgroup content.

13. You and the steering team will need to decide who will present the material in Chapters 2, 3, and 4. All the content can be presented by the facilitator, some by a second person, or each of the three chapters by a different person.

    We also recommend that you secure a Microsoft® Word diskette copy of the text so that you can edit the wording to better fit each presenter's language style. You can also change the type style and font to a size more conducive to being presented or read. (See Appendix G to order.)

    It is best if the presenter knows the content well enough that using the PowerPoint® or overhead projector slide is sufficient to communicate the information.

14. We encourage you to use the Microsoft® PowerPoint® visuals also available on the diskette. They can be projected using an LCD projector, or printed onto transparencies and used with an overhead projector.

15. During the event, you or someone from the congregation or steering team, will need to modify the draft wording of the constitution provided in Appendix B to match the decisions made in the Chapter 6 session. Those revisions need to be entered during lunch or the first part of the afternoon. If you are making the changes, make them during lunch. You will want to be available to the subgroups during the first part of the afternoon.

16. Frequently monitor the clock. Be aware of where you are in relation to the schedule. Getting behind early creates significant issues later in the afternoon. It is better to be a bit directive early than to need an additional hour at the end.

17. Help the steering team understand that the final session is greatly aided by the ability to project draft wording on a screen so that everyone can see. It gives you as facilitator the opportunity to help inject words and

phrases that will complete discussions and keep the meeting moving.

18. Help the steering team understand that the material presented in Chapters 2, 3, and 4 must be presented to the assembly. Taking the time to present those insights will greatly shorten the time needed to adopt the church's version of the model constitution and bylaws. The material gives everyone a common vocabulary. When people who are concerned about achieving the Great Commission are aware of the realities churches face in current times, they eagerly approve new structures to make that ministry happen.

19. If the assembly is split with perhaps twenty-five percent or fewer on one side of an issue, declare it a "preliminary decision" to be reviewed at a later time, after everyone has had some time to think about it. Keep moving.

20. If the assembly is split with perhaps forty percent on one side of an issue, indicate that this matter will be investigated further and again discussed at a later date. You and the steering team will have to determine if the matter is substantial, requiring in-depth discussion.

    If so, we recommend creating an action team made up of everyone who wants to serve. That team is given not more than four weeks to reach closure on recommended wording. In the end, it may be necessary in the final stages of the constitutional change process to simply vote on a wording of one section and then submit the entire draft for approval. It is extremely unusual for any one point to become a "deal breaker," blocking approval of the new constitution and bylaws.

21. Help the steering team find a way to celebrate the accomplishment of drafting a new document. The event will create momentum to the entire ministry. The steering team can help the church's leaders capture and continue that momentum.

The event to create a new constitution and bylaws is a powerful way for the entire congregation to actively energize its ministry. You will feel a sense of reward for your efforts at making this event a success.

www.MissionGrowth.org – click "Publishing"

Diskette for the *Flexible, Missional Constitution/Bylaws* event

- 3½ inch diskette
- IBM PC or equivalent
- Licensed for use at one congregation per diskette purchased
- Microsoft® Word 97 or later files
  - Constitution and Bylaws of St. Paul Church (Appendix A)
  - Draft Constitution and Bylaws (Appendix B)
  - Presentation text script of Chapters 2, 3, 4, and 6
  - Notes to subgroups and other wordings (Appendix C, D, and E)
  - Draft of policies for boards, committees, task forces, action teams, etc.
- PowerPoint® 97 or later files
  - Presentation slides for content in Chapters 2, 3, 4, and 6

Also available from *Mission Growth Publishing:*

Quiet Conversations: Concrete Help for Weary Ministry Leaders

In the United States, about 100,000 parish pastors (and their families) are experiencing career burnout. *Quiet Conversations* follows Pastor Paul and his spouse Kristin as they come to understand what has gone wrong and discover a way back to personal and ministry health. Feel the hurts they experience but do not share with their congregation's leaders—or anyone else. Experience the release that comes from admitting trouble and seeking help. Share their joy as they discover hope for the future.

"This is a terrific book. It actually embodies what it proposes. The main points are right on. This is a book I think most pastors should read. I am going to distribute it widely."
- **Speed Leas, congregation conflict author and consultant**

"What the future parish pastor (and spouse) is not taught in seminary must be learned later, often painfully. Sometimes pain causes the victim to leave the ministry. One alternative is to read *Quiet Conversations.*"
- **Lyle Schaller, dean of congregation consultants**

In Search of the Unchurched: The Difference Between Thriving and Struggling Churches

In Search of the Unchurched offers a way to discuss the changes affecting mainline denominations and local congregation. This book is designed to help congregations explore the factual truths about what was and what is as a way to motivate discussion about what is working and what's not working. You'll discover how congregations wrestled with the same issues you are facing (ministry to current members, ministry to unchurched, worship, changing neighborhoods, and more).

"This book needs to be read and used by every church who is at all concerned about reaching the unchurched. I say 'read and used' because the book can be used for self-study. Dr. Klaas includes periodic Action Suggestions and discussion questions. Thanks for this important book."
- **Dave Anderson, president of The Fellowship Ministries**